■SCHOLASTIC

PHOTOS of
201 TEACHER-CREATED
CHARTS

by Mary Beth Spann

NEW YORK • TORONTO • LONDON • AUCKLAND • SYDNEY
MEXICO CITY • NEW DELHI • HONG KONG • BUENOS AIRES

Teaching
Resources

Dedication

With great gratitude to educator and child champion Jack Schwartz, who never said no to my ideas.

And to teachers everywhere who work hard to make classroom charts that teach, motivate, and inspire.

Acknowledgments

I am most appreciative to the principals of seven elementary schools
representing five separate school districts located in Suffolk County, Long Island, NY:

These dedicated professionals enthusiastically supported my efforts to complete this book by allowing me access to their schools' classrooms so I could photograph the collection of charts displayed there.

Shoreham-Wading River School District

Briarcliff Elementary School,
Ms. Liala Strotman, Principal

Miller Avenue School,
Mr. Jack Schwartz, Principal

Wading River Elementary School,
Mr. Stephen Donohue, Principal

Eastport/South Manor School District

South Street School,
Robin Barbera, Principal

Longwood Central School District

Ridge Elementary School,
Janine Rozycki, Principal

West Middle Island Elementary School,
Wynstelle Nicholson, Principal

Miller Place Union Free School District

Andrew Mueller Primary School,
Karen Reichert, Principal

Also many thanks to the following teachers* representing the above school districts.
These teachers kindly allowed me to photograph the creative charts displayed in their classrooms.
Without their willingness to open their classrooms to me, this book would not have been possible.

Connie Albin	Kelly Darcy	Rose Hill	Regina Luckas	Jackie Reyling
Pierrette Alexandre	Kerri Darcy	Susan Hommel	Jen Ogden	Carol Quierolo
Kerri Anderson	Jackie Deangelo	Carol Jackson	Maureen Madigan	Cindy Schafer
Pauline Auch	Malia Devincenzo	Joan Jacobs	Christine Maniaci	Kristin Scharf
Cynthia Austin	Lauren Diecco	Ralph Jimenez	Nancy Mare	Tracy Southerland
Jennifer Arroyo	Laura Donahue	Lorrie Keeley	Jacqueline M. Margraf	Kathy Starke
Paula Athanasopoulos	Caroline Dowling	Kathy Kerr	Susan Markee	Maureen Taculli
Judy Baker	Irene Drake	Mary Beth Kessler	Rose Mcguire	Tara Verunac
Missy Bobal	Scott Dippel	Michelle King	Gina Moreno	Tonia Villano
Stephen Burns	Leah Fabbricante	Stacia Klefsky	Elizabeth Moskowitz	Linda Vitale
Ann Bucco	Kristin Ferrante	Noelle Kouris	Kristen Murray	Kerri Weiss
Patricia Calone	Karen Filalkowsky	Alison Krieb	Melissa Nasslan	Christina Wolcson
Salley Castoro	Paul Ganci	Kerri Langan	Jennifer Nichols	Lind Wygonik
Jessica Clemente	Peggy Giacomin	Laurette Laprarie	Mary Lynn Orgonas	Patricia Young
Kelly Coleman	Renee Gilmore	Judith Laz	Debbie Omisore	
Jerri Cotter	Kathy Hanley	Deborah Lilly	Sue Ann Rea	
Jean Dalecki	Dawn Hibbard	Kassy Lock	Pat Remel	

*Please know every effort was made to secure every contributor's name. If anyone was overlooked, please accept our sincere apologies. Know, too, that name or no name, your contribution is invaluable as it helps students and teachers everywhere continue their growth and learning.

Cover design by Jason Robinson
Interior design by Solas

ISBN-13 978-0-439-24312-4
ISBN-10 0-439-24312-2

Copyright © 2008 by Mary Beth Spann
All rights reserved. Printed in the U.S.A.

2 3 4 5 6 7 8 9 10   40   15 14 13 12 11 10 09 08

TABLE OF CONTENTS

THE CHARTS

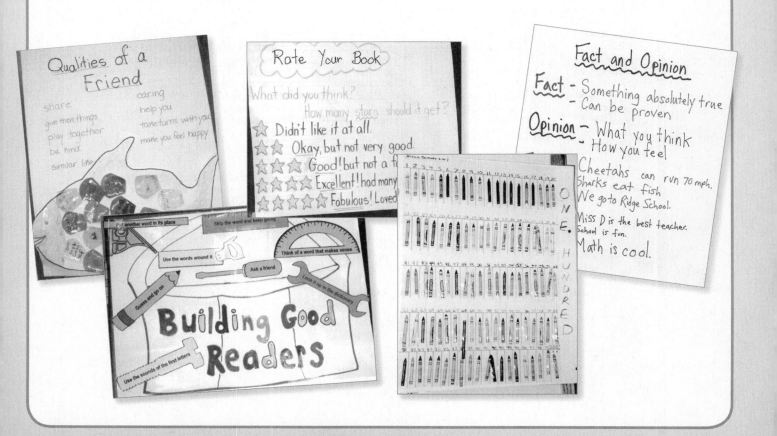

INTRODUCTION

The book you hold in your hands is a resource you will come to value and depend on. It features a host of powerful and meaningful cross-curricular charts developed by teachers like you, for and with their students. The charts in this book were collected from classrooms in seven elementary schools in Suffolk County, Long Island, New York. The charts are all educationally sound, purposeful, meaningful, and thoroughly classroom-tested. Best of all, they really, really work!

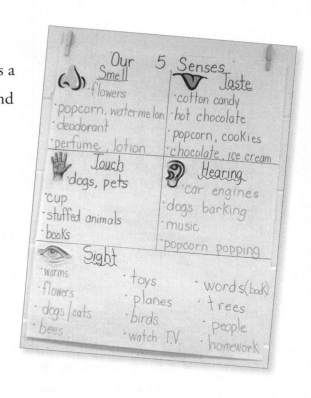

Let this book inspire you to create charts to suit the needs of all your students. Take notice of the materials the teachers used, the way they displayed and organized information, and the reasons they made the charts in the first place. Then let your imagination soar. You'll soon be charting your way to learning success in your classroom.

WHY USE CHARTS IN THE CLASSROOM?

We're all influenced by the print that surrounds us every day. The words we see displayed send messages that help spark ideas, make connections, broaden vocabularies, and make room for new ways of thinking and viewing the world.

After visiting the classrooms featured in this book, I have come to view classroom charts as "silent teaching partners." These partners cost pennies to create, but they dispense a wealth of guidance, information, warmth, and wisdom whenever and wherever needed in your classroom.

Here are a few more reasons to begin using charts in your classroom:

✔ Charts can be teacher-made, student-made, or developed as a cooperative, interactive effort between you and your students.

✔ Charts offer flexibility and can be developed all at once or created slowly over time.

✔ When contributing to charts, children have an opportunity to arrange and sort information in a variety of ways.

✔ Charts can inform, direct, and inspire. They can help children find ways to learn more effectively and solve their own problems.

✔ Charts can entertain and amuse.

✔ Charts serve up information in logical, digestible amounts.

✔ Charts can address any and all areas of the curriculum.

✔ Charts can help you manage your classroom. They can be used to list expectations, spell out routines, and offer students step-by-step guidance for how to proceed independently through a process or activity.

✔ Charts provide a meaningful reading/writing experience.

✔ Interactive charts demonstrate tolerance and respect for different ideas.

✔ Charts can be used to boost self-esteem and to generate a positive classroom climate.

✔ When children contribute information and ideas to a chart, they enjoy a sense of ownership over their own learning.

HOW TO USE THIS BOOK

The charts in this book are divided into four basic sections:

I. Classroom management   **3.** Math

2. Literacy   **4.** Science (and more)

You will, however, discover some overlap. For example, a math chart can support your literacy goals, and a science chart can double as a math chart.

Classroom Management Charts: These charts are designed to help organize and direct the activities in your classroom. In this section you'll find charts to help welcome children to your class, establish routines, as well as spell out classroom rules and expectations.

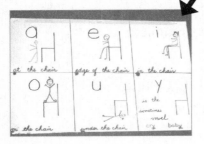

Literacy Charts: Literacy charts help foster skills and concepts related to print awareness, reading, writing, and spelling, as well as organizing and directing independent reading and writing programs. There are even charts to help children manage their own literacy challenges, such as how to choose a book, what to do when they come to a word they can't read, or how to get unstuck when they can't think of a writing topic. You'll find an assortment of editing checklist charts, writing tip-sheet charts, and writing prompt charts . . . plus many more.

Math Charts: The charts in this section help children make sense of math vocabulary, skills, and operations. It includes a number of charts for helping children learn how to create and read graphs, as well as charts for counting up to the 100th day of school.

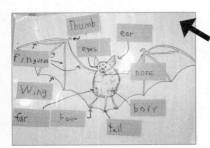

Science Charts and More: Here you'll find science charts that deliver and review science concepts such as colors, weather, the five senses, and concepts related to health and safety. In addition, you'll find several more great charts that serve to round out this whole collection.

Throughout the book you'll also see Terrific Tips for maximizing the teaching and learning potential available with each chart model.

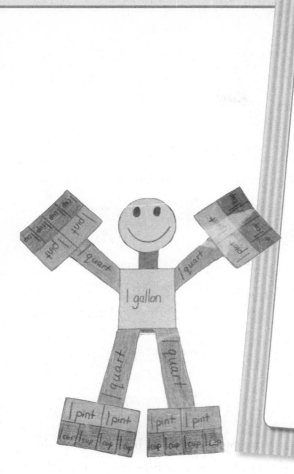

GETTING STARTED WITH TEACHING CHARTS

It's easy to begin using charts in your classroom. All you need are a few supplies and a willingness to get started.

Basic Construction, Design and Display Tips

Throughout this book you'll find lots of ideas for creating great charts, but here are the most important points to keep in mind:

1. The goal of any chart is to display information. The best charts, therefore, display information in a clear, uncluttered, easy-to-read fashion.

2. Record information with colored markers to highlight important words and phrases. You can underline key words or print them with a marker of a contrasting color. You can also try alternating colors so children reading from a distance can more easily track which line they're reading.

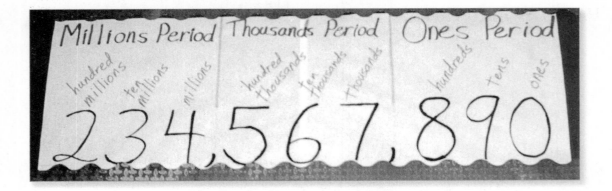

3. Keep it BIG. Use large, clear lettering on your charts. A chart created with small, cramped lettering is unreadable from a distance. Such a chart is useless to children who can't see it. Also, if you have a lot of content, better to tape two or more sheets of chart paper together rather than trying to cram all the information onto a single page.

4. Display each chart at children's eye level, in the particular spot in the room where each chart is most likely to be used. For example, post your writer's checklist chart in your writing workshop area, and your list of fire drill rules near your exit door.

5. For charts that present a lot of text, alternate two or more colors, so no two lines are written in the same hue. This technique makes such charts much easier to read.

6. Use a heavy-stock paper to create any charts you plan on using from year to year, then laminate for extra durability.

7. Use chart paper to record brainstorming sessions and for interactive charts that you will likely want to create fresh with each new class. Laminate any you want to display all year long.

8. Always use positive language to express your charts' messages. For example, when making a list of class guidelines, create a list of desired behaviors rather than a list of behaviors students should avoid.

9. Listen to children's questions and complaints. Those that surface again and again (e.g., *I don't know what to write about, I don't know how to spell a word, I'm all done,* and *What do I do now?*) can be addressed by creating charts that offer information to help children learn to direct themselves.

BASIC CHART MODELS

Here is just a partial list of basic charts you can display in your classroom:

✓ Daily Schedule Chart

✓ Attendance Chart

✓ Lunch Choice Chart

✓ Job Chart

✓ Good Listening Rules

✓ Learning Centers Assignment Chart

✓ Handwriting Helper Chart

✓ How-To Charts

✓ Literacy Charts (fostering alphabet awareness, word study, reading, spelling and writing, and so on)

✓ Computer Literacy Charts

✓ Writing and Editing Charts

✓ Number Charts

✓ Pattern Charts

✓ Mathematical Operations Charts

✓ Health Charts

✓ Emergency Procedure Charts

✓ Organizational Guidelines Charts

✓ Homework Helper Charts

✓ Personal Goal Charts

✓ Famous Quotation Charts

winter words

gloves scarf

snow   flurries
snowballs   igloo
snowflakes
blizzard   cold
skiing   icy
shiver
snowman   icicles
sledding   skating
snowboarding   angels
snowmobile   hot cocoa
snowcones   snow plow
fireplace   frostbite
freezing   frozen
soup   jacket   hat
mittens   boots

MAKING THE MOST OF TEACHING CHARTS

Once you make the effort to create your classroom charts, you'll want to make sure you squeeze every last drop of teaching and learning potential from each one. Here's how:

Involve children as much as possible in the chart-making process.

The more they have invested in a chart and the more interactive the experience of creating a chart is, the more children will relate to the information it displays.

Create charts that are colorful and pleasant to view.

Your charts do not have to be works of art, but small touches like stickers, glitter glue, drawn-on icons and borders, and magazine pictures go a long way toward enhancing any chart. Children are usually eager to add personal touches; student photos and illustrations are particular favorites.

When children ask questions already answered on a chart, direct them to that chart.

Resist the urge to answer children's inquiries directly when the issues have already been addressed on a chart. Instead, remind them that there are ways to solve the problem on their own—and that those ways are listed on one or more charts in the room.

Rotate and refresh charts frequently.

With time, even the most compelling charts lose impact. If a chart has worn out its welcome, replace it with a new one. If a chart contains information you wish to display all year long, consider having the children help you recycle the information by creating a new chart with the old message. Or, have children volunteer to make mini-posters of each point on the chart so you can display the same information in a fresh way.

Make reproducible versions of checklist charts.

Any time you create a chart that offers children information for self-evaluation or self-checking, consider making a reproducible version of the chart. Then, offer each child a copy of the chart so he or she can access the information anywhere, even at home.

1 Welcome to Our Classroom!

This charming chart serves as a warm welcome to parents visiting their child's classroom on Back to School Night. Print the greeting across the top of the chart paper (or have children use their cooperative writing skills to create this message) and then have children use different-colored markers to sign their names to the message. Variations include: "Welcome to Our Classroom!" "We Welcome You to Ms./Mr. _____'s Class!" and "Our Class Welcomes Friends and Family!"

2 Daily Count-Up and Sign-In

This chart invites children to sign themselves in to class as they count the first 100 days of school. Create numbered blank spaces on a sheet of chart paper (one for each child you're expecting on the first day of class). At the top of the chart, print a cheerful welcome message inviting children to your classroom. Add the date and which day this represents in the school year (e.g., "Happy 1st Day of School!") Post your chart at the children's eye level or place on a table near the entrance to your classroom. Have a marker on hand so children can sign in as they arrive.

Terrific Tips: Laminate your chart and have children sign in using a dry erase marker. Preprint each child's name in pencil on the chart. Help each child locate his or her name, and then have each child use the marker to trace over his or her name.

That's What Friends Do!

Friends care about each other.

Friends share.

Friends help each other.

Friends protect each other.

Friends are kind.

Friends listen to each other.

3 That's What Friends Do

Encourage students to suggest ways they can befriend each other. In addition to transcribing ideas from students—*Friends share, Friends help each other*—let them use collaborative writing to record their suggestions. (Look closely and you'll see how a bit of white tape helped correct errors on the chart above so that all spelling and punctuation meets conventional standards.)

4 School Bus Bar Graph

Trace a small bus shape several times onto a piece of copy paper. Then reproduce and cut out one for each child. Invite children to print their names on the bus and color it. Use a piece of chart paper to list the bus lines the children will be taking home. You can also include a row for children who get picked up by car, and a row for those who walk home. Have each child place his or her bus on the chart to create a graph.

> **Terrific Tip:** Ask, "Which bus has the least number of students from this class? The most? How many students travel home other ways?"

5 Class Rules and Agreements

To create an evolving class rules chart, use sentence strips and a simple sentence starter, "We agree that . . ." This allows the class to create new rules and "agreements" over time.

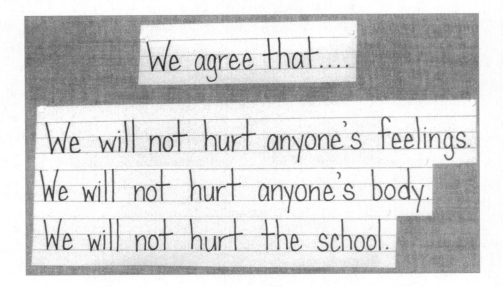

6 How Can We Make This a Great Classroom?

Begin by posing the question, "How can we make this a great classroom?" Then help children brainstorm a list of answers to provide a list of meaningful class rules. Children automatically understand the rationale for each rule, because each one answers the original question!

Be Helpful, Not Hurtful
We can be helpful by...
· talk out fights, tell a teacher
· Sharing
· Help people, tell a teacher if hurt
· Use manners, be nice
· Entertain/welcome new kids
· Take turns, raise your hand
· Have patience
· Rule of 1
· Don't hurt bodies or feelings

7 Motto Motivation

Top your list of class rules with an easy-to-remember class slogan or motto. The students who helped create this chart chose the motto "Be Helpful, Not Hurtful" to head up their list of guidelines. Use this motto, or create one of your own.

8 Our Class Rules

This charming chart is composed of simple, child-generated one- and two-word guidelines recorded on sentence strips, which are then attached to chart paper. Have children sign their names to seal the agreement.

Our Class Rules
Be KinD   Listen
TaKE TurNs Share
CLeaN uP   SMile☺
ASK Questions

Emma♥
rob   HOlly   philip
          MacKENZIE   Dani
                Alex HAYDNNICK Kevin
Katie   Mike   Michaella
ERIN
          Mikey NataLie

9 School of Fish Rules

After crafting your list of classroom rules, cut out paper fish and offer each child one to personalize. Display your list and your "School of Fish" together on a blue "underwater" background, as shown here.

Terrific Tip: To freshen the display, offer children a series of different seasonal shapes to personalize.

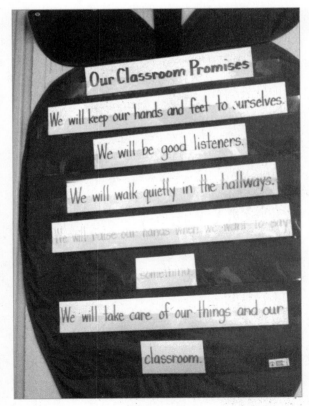

10 Pocket Chart Promises

Reframe the idea of rules altogether: instead of asking children to follow rules, this chart encourages children to keep classroom "promises." Use an apple-shaped pocket chart and sentence strips with promises printed in different-colored markers. The result is a display that's appealing and easy to read.

Terrific Tip: This chart is easy to modify, freshen, and customize. If you want to remind children of positive behaviors for a field trip or fire drill, simply substitute a new promise (or two or three)!

11 Qualities of a Friend

For young learners, the essence of positive behavior is friendship. With friendship as the theme of this chart, you can easily remind children that school friends are always eager to help each other learn and grow.

> **Terrific Tip:** Support this theme by reading books with your class on the value of friendship.

12 Class Motto: Mutual Respect

This simple but elegant class motto says it all. Class members (and the teacher, too) can measure every thought and action against its powerful message.

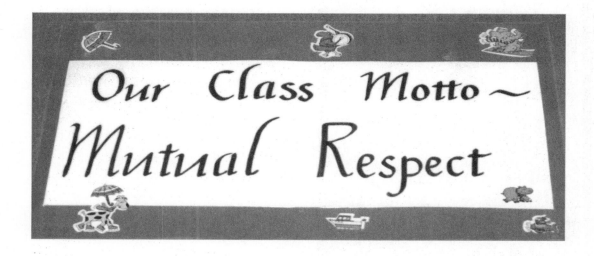

13 Good-Behavior Chart

For this chart, choose any desired behavior you wish to foster in your students. Then on a sheet of chart paper, give a definition of the behavior. Leave room underneath for children to list ways they will practice the behavior in their daily lives. For example, on the chart shown here, the teacher defined "self-control," and then students offered concrete ways they would put this behavior into practice.

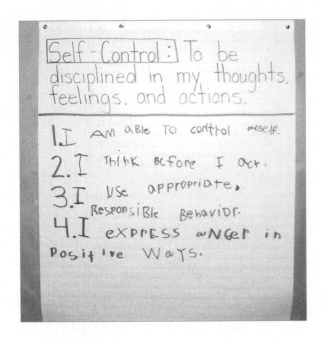

14 Craft-Stick Job Center

Print children's names on craft sticks. Then glue small, correspondence-size envelopes to oaktag, and label each one with the name of a class job. If desired, decorate envelopes with a symbol relating to each job (e.g., a picture of books for the library monitor). Assign jobs by placing craft sticks in the appropriate envelopes.

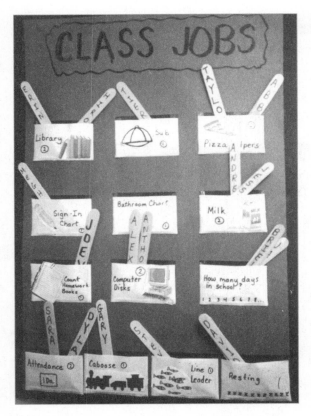

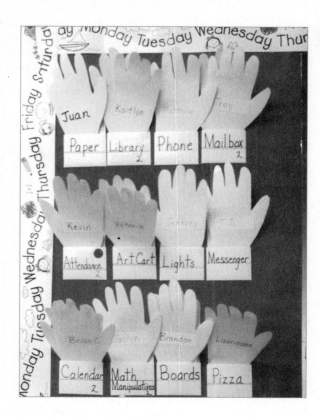

15 Handy Jobs

Here's a job chart that symbolizes the age-old adage "Many hands make light work!" First, trace a hand shape (including wrist) onto oaktag or discarded file folders. Make one hand for each student and label each with a child's name. Next, cut sentence strips into segments slightly longer than the width of the paper wrists. Label these strips with the names of various classroom jobs you want the children to share. Glue the strips to a large piece of oaktag, leaving the top unglued to create a pocket. Assign class jobs by placing the hands in the appropriate pockets. Rotate responsibilities by rotating hands into different pockets.

> **Terrific Tip:** Include one extra (unlabeled) pocket for storing hands when they're not assigned to a job.

16 Easy Morning Message

This morning message is easy and packed with learning for emerging and beginning readers. The note is only two sentences long (not counting the salutation and closing) and is written with key beginning and ending letters missing. Invite students to fill in the blank spaces with the correct letters so the message makes sense. You can also leave out punctuation marks for students to fill in. Students can take turns being responsible for completing this daily task or you can present this activity as a group effort to kick off your daily circle time. As the year goes on, you can prepare more complex messages (with whole words missing) for students to complete.

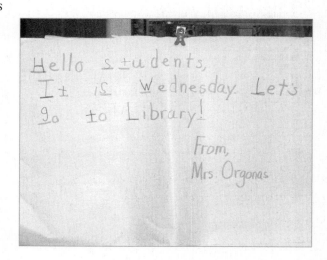

17 Greeting and Skills Review

This morning greeting doubles as the first activity of the day! Create a fill-in-the-blank morning message that lets you review material children have already covered. You might want to keep the first few fill-ins the same each day, and add new ones below. In the chart shown here, for example, the teacher posed the same first four fill-ins (related to the day and date) again and again but changed the rest.

Terrific Tip: Although this sample chart relates to math, you can plug in any activity you wish.

18 Morning Message Mistakes

This good-morning message chart is irresistible because it gives students a chance to hunt down your writing "mistakes." Try incorporating errors involving letter formations, spellings, word choice, and punctuation. Then let your student editors proofread and correct your work.

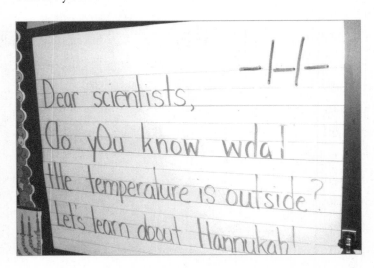

> Dear boys and girls,
> I hope you have a wonderful day with Mrs Abaddo.
> You have Library, Music and Sing A Long today.
> Love,
> Mrs. Sprazano

19 While You Were Out . . .

When you plan to be away for the day, connect with your students by way of a cheerful morning message chart. Your message can introduce the substitute teacher and review the day's activities.

20 Today, Yesterday, Tomorrow

Here's a great chart for exploring calendar vocabulary that we often presume children understand. Create the chart shown here and laminate or cover with clear self-adhesive paper. Each day assign one student to first erase the information recorded the day before and then to use a dry erase marker to update the chart so it reflects the current day's information. Read the information together as a class. This chart works well as you count up to the 100th day of school—and beyond!

> Today is _Wed._ , _June_ _14th_ _2004_ .
> Yesterday was _Tues._ .
> Tomorrow will be _Thurs_ .
> We've had _169_ days of school.

21 Color-Coded Centers

Assign a color to each learning center or activity area in your classroom. Create a chart that displays the names of the centers, and beside each name, add a large paper circle in the appropriate color along with a small picture cue. Use self-sticking colored dots (purchased at an office-supply store) to label books, materials, and supplies so students can easily tell which objects belong in which center. This color-coded system makes clean-up a snap!

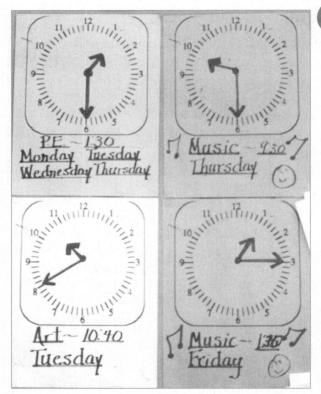

22 Daily Schedule Clocks

Draw simple analog clocks on different-colored pieces of oaktag—one clock for each special activity your class participates in (e.g., music, physical education, and so on). Draw hands on the clocks indicating the time each activity is scheduled. Beneath each clock, list the days that activity takes place.

> **Terrific Tip:** If an activity takes place on different days at different times, create different clocks, but use the same color.

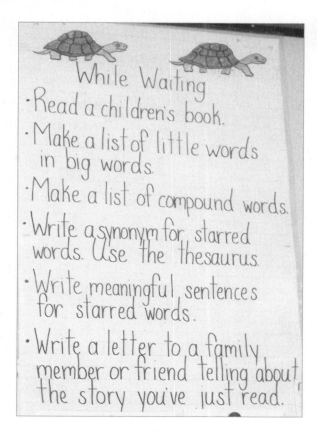

23 While Waiting

This chart lets students know that "wait-time" is not wasted time. Students can fill these in-between times with meaningful activities as they wait for one activity to end and another to begin. List ideas such as "Read a book" and "Make a list of little words in big words." Consider changing the chart from time to time to keep ideas fresh.

24 Good Test-Taking Skills

Help students become self-directing when taking tests. This simple but effective chart serves to remind them of steps they can take to maximize their chances for test-taking success.

> **Terrific Tip:** Different test-taking skills are required for different types of tests. Consider generating an assortment of charts customized to fit your various testing formats and requirements.

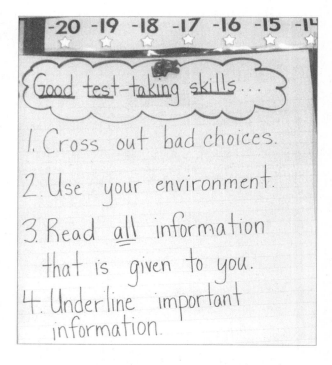

25 Birthday Balloons

To make this birthday chart, cut 12 balloon shapes from colorful paper, and label each balloon with a month of the year. Add yarn strings. On each balloon, list the names and dates of children celebrating birthdays that month. Then on each child's big day, have the class autograph a separate paper balloon for the birthday child to take home.

26 Birthday Teddy Bears

Offer each child a paper teddy bear with an oval cut-out in the center. Provide art supplies (yarn, sequins, buttons) so children can decorate their bears. Place students' photos in their teddy bear frames. Then use chart paper to draw a grid. List the months of the school year down the left-hand side of the grid. Next to each month, display the bears of the children whose birthdays fall in that month.

27 Birthdays to Celebrate

Use sentence strips to print each month of the year and attach them in order to a piece of oaktag. Next to each month, display photos of the children whose birthdays fall in that month.

> **Terrific Tip:** Place photos face down on the display. At the start of each month, turn that month's collection of photos over to reveal the faces of the birthday children.

28 Textured Alphabet Frieze

To create this series of textured 3-D alphabet mini-charts (that combine to make a large alphabet display), enlist the help of students and their families. Send each child home with a plain, undecorated alphabet letter. Have them fill the inside of their letter with something—objects or pictures—whose name begins with that letter. The result? A textured alphabet chart featuring such clever ideas as *Bb*'s covered in buttons, *Dd*'s covered in play dollar bills, and *Zz*'s decorated with real zippers!

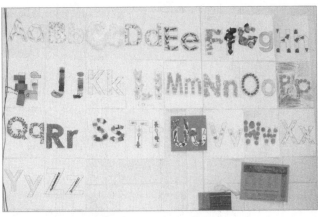

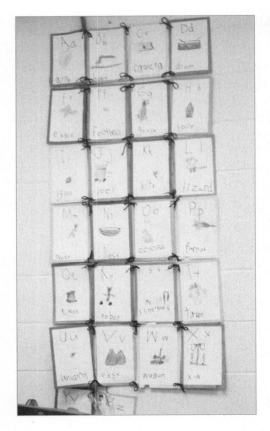

29 Alphabet Quilt

Each quilt block in this chart is simply a plain piece of copy paper mounted on construction paper. To create the blocks, assign each student a letter and have them follow this format: First, print the upper- and lowercase letter at the top of the block. Next, draw a picture of an object beginning with that letter. Finally, record the name of the object beneath the picture. (You may want to model these steps for children before they begin.)

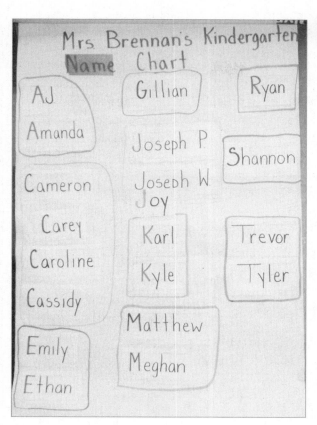

30 Name Word Wall

To make this name word wall, print each student's name on a piece of primary-lined chart paper. Use a different-colored marker to print the first letters of names sharing the same first letter (e.g., a red marker for names beginning with A, a green marker for names beginning with B, and so on). Cut the names apart and place them on a piece of oaktag, grouped by beginning letter. Outline each set of names using a marker in a color that matches the names.

31 Meet Our Classmates Charts

As a beginning-of-the-year writing project, have each child answer a series of personal questions (e.g., What is your name? How old are you? Do you have brothers or sisters? What kinds of pets do you own?). Help children use their answers to craft third-person biographies designed to introduce themselves to the class. Copy the finished biographies onto chart paper. After sharing the charts aloud, display them around the room.

Meet Dominic

Dominic is 6 years old. He has one sister named Samantha. He has one dog named Jazz and its a pug. His other dog is named Angus and it is a black lab. He loves macaroni and cheese, and Play Station 2.

32 Weekly Spelling Word Wall

Use solid-colored corrugated border paper to section off a portion of a larger bulletin board that you've already covered with bright, solid-colored craft paper. Use this space to post spelling or vocabulary word cards for the week.

Terrific Tip: Save your word cards in dated envelopes and reuse when appropriate from year to year.

33 Fall Words Chart

Use markers in autumnal colors to create a fall word wall featuring words associated with autumn. You can create the chart yourself or invite children to offer ideas as you transcribe them.

Terrific Tip: Make a word chart for each month or season of the school year.

34 Five Senses Autumn Poem

This chart helps children connect to all five senses. Each line of the poem begins with the word "Autumn" followed by a sensory connection. (Autumn feels like . . . , Autumn tastes like . . . , Autumn sounds like . . . , and so on).

Autumn

Autumn feels like cold winter.

Autumn tastes like a Thanksgiving feast that is being eaten

Autumn sounds like crunching leaves.

Autumn looks like colorful leaves falling off the bare trees.

Autumn smells like apple pie being baked in an oven.

Terrific Tip: As a chart poem, this sensory model lends itself well to any experience the children share together.

35 Words of the Month

Represent every month with a different-colored banner cut from lengths of seasonal-colored craft paper (green for September, orange for October, brown for November, red for December, and so on). Have children make symbols of the month—miniature art projects created from construction paper scraps—and glue them to the banner and then label with collaborative writing. Then hang the banners side-by-side from ceiling wire. Displayed in this way, the banner charts remind children of all they've learned and celebrated during the year.

36 Seasonal Word Wall

Use a simple shape—such as the snowman pictured here—to feature seasonal words children can read and copy in their own writing. To complete your display, surround your word wall shape with related crafts (such as the student-designed snowflakes shown here) or student-generated seasonal writings. Other seasonal shapes you can use include a school bus for Back to School and balloons or a bouquet of flowers for spring.

winter words

gloves   scarf

snow   flurries
snowballs   igloo
snowflakes
blizzard   cold
skiing   icy
shiver
snowman   icicles
sledding   skating
snowboarding   angels
snowmobile   hot cocoa
snowcones   snow plow
fireplace   frostbite
freezing   frozen
soup   jacket   hat
mittens   boots

37 Winter Wonderland

Have students use collaborative writing to record the lyrics to the popular tune "Winter Wonderland." You can use the same idea to turn any set of song lyrics into an interactive collaborative writing chart.

Terrific Tip: Embellish the chart by having children fashion "snow globes" of themselves. To do this, students mount wintry digital photos of themselves on paper circles brushed with "diamond dust."

Sleigh bells ring,
are you listening?
In the lane, snow is
glistening.
A beautiful sight,
we're happy tonight,
walking in a
winter wonderland!

38 Five Little Fishies

Use sticky notes to highlight the word *said*, which recurs in each line of this favorite children's song. By doing this, the repetition, rhythm, and patterns of the poem became apparent. On another day, you might choose to highlight the ordinal numbers in the poem, or another repeated word, such as *the* or *one*. Or, you may decide to have students substitute another word for *said*, such as *exclaimed* or *whispered*.

39 Field Trip Memories

This chart recounts one class's experiences on a field trip. After writing the chart with students, the teacher used a marker in a contrasting color to circle target sight words.

> **Terrific Tip:** Invite student volunteers to come up and print select words on the chart. Adding to the print or graphics on a chart is one way students can feel ownership of the content.

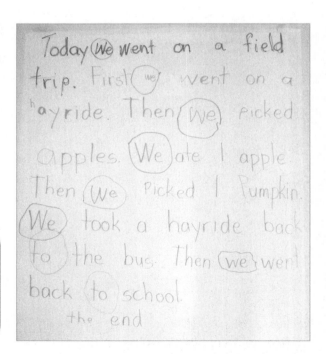

40 Words That Begin Like "Louis"

Create a chart for each child in the class, featuring words that begin with the same letter as his or her name. The charts can remain up all year long, and you can add new words as they are harvested from oral and written activities. At the end of the year, present the personalized charts to each child as a keepsake.

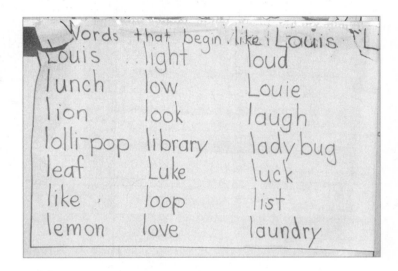

41 Letter List

Create lists like the one shown here for each consonant in the alphabet. Invite children to take turns adding small line illustrations to any words they choose. This interactive element helps children remember the words and adds charm to the chart.

42 Gooey Gumdrops

Use highlighting tape to emphasize the upper- and lowercase version of one particular letter in a poem or passage. If you choose to highlight two different letters, use two different colors of tape. As students read the passage, have them emphasize the target letter's sound before you remove the tape from that word. Later you can reread the passage again, emphasizing each word containing the target letter(s) and have students reapply the tape to the letter(s) as you go.

Gumdrops
Gooey, gooey gumdrops,
they are so good.
I would gobble one
everyday,
if my mommy said I could!

43 Short-Vowel Stick Figures

The stick figure drawings on this chart provide children with visual cues that help them easily recall the short-vowel sounds. To make, divide a piece of oaktag into six even segments. Label each segment as shown here. For each label, draw a corresponding stick figure and chair as shown.

Terrific Tip: Have students refer to the poster as they "act out" the vowel sounds at their chairs.

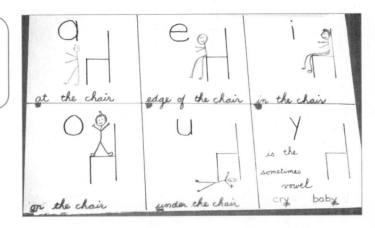

44 Vowels in Our Names

Sort students' names according to the vowels contained in each. To make this chart, divide a piece of chart paper into five columns and label the columns A, E, I, O and U (make six columns if you want to include Y). Have children examine their names to identify the vowels they contain, and then print them in one or more corresponding vowel columns. For example, the name "Pat" would appear in the column marked A, while "Paul" would appear in the A column and the U column.

Terrific Tip: Use the chart to count the number of names that contain each vowel or the number of vowels in each name.

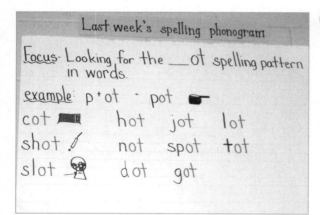

45 Last Week's Spelling Phonogram

A simple sentence strip transforms last week's spelling phonogram chart into this week's spelling phonogram review chart. The chart itself is clear; it offers a sample sentence containing the phonogram and provides small drawings to illustrate some of the words. Be sure to print each featured phonogram in a contrasting color so students can really pay attention to it.

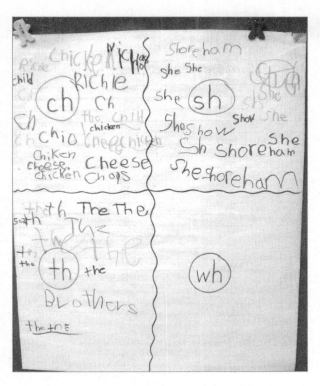

46 Digraph Sort

Divide a piece of chart paper into four equal sections. Place one consonant digraph in each section. Challenge children to harvest words containing each digraph and to print them in the appropriate segments on the chart.

> **Terrific Tip:** You may want to introduce one digraph at a time, adding others to the chart over time.

47 Word Family Chart

This chart features one word-family ending (in this case, -*ash*) and a list of words containing that ending. The beauty of this chart is that once children can read the word ending, they can easily read all the words. In addition, the words rhyme so children can easily incorporate them into real and nonsensical rhyming poems, stories, and wordplay.

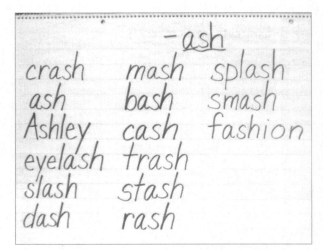

48 Word Family List

Recycle your unused bulletin board pieces as word-family chart toppers. Use a marker to label each piece with an appropriate letter cluster or ending. Then attach a length of chart paper cut into strips to each topper. Use different-colored markers to create each list of words containing the target letter sound. If desired, use a contrasting color of marker to underline the target letters in each word.

49 Good Readers

Just what makes a "good reader" anyway? This chart helps students understand in concrete terms what exactly a good reader is. To create the chart, list the attributes shown here, or provide your own.

Good Readers...

• know or understand what they're reading

• choose appropriate books.
  not too hard

• make predictions, ask questions.
  I think...   What's happening here?

• reread if they are confused.

• make pictures in mind.

Terrific Tip: Use a marker in a contrasting color to define difficult vocabulary, as shown.

50 Decoding Tools

This chart likens reading skills to handy tools ready for use when children reach a word they cannot read. To create the chart, trace real tools on colorful pieces of construction or craft paper. Cut the tools out and glue them to a sheet of chart paper on which you've drawn a simple tool apron.

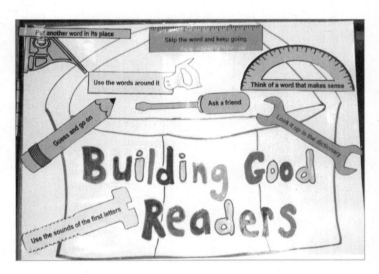

51 What Do We Like to Read About?

This chart personalizes students' reading achievements by pairing names with favorite titles or subjects. The chart offers students a way to share their interests with others and gives you a glimpse into independent-reading interests and abilities. You might want to challenge children to each choose a title inspired by another classmate's reading. You can then create a companion list of the new titles read.

What does Mrs. Weiss Class like to read about?
Jenna- Ghostville Elementary
Ian- Lego helicopter, Soccer, Poetry
Jamie- Poetry, Pyramids
Shannon- Flat Stanley
Ricky- Sharks, Planets
Myhayla- Horses, Eric Carle (Grouchy Ladybug)
Imani- Ready Freddy, Junie B. Jones
Elijah- Bats, T-Rex
Gary- Baseball Sports, Sponge Bob
Madison- Puppies, Magic Tricks
Samantha- I Spy, Care Bears
Brandon- Dinosaurs, Magazines

52 When You Read . . .

Use sentence strips to create a chart that offers strategies students can keep in mind as they read. To make the chart, include the suggestions shown here, or offer some of your own. As students' reading skills evolve, replace older sentence strips with new, more advanced skills.

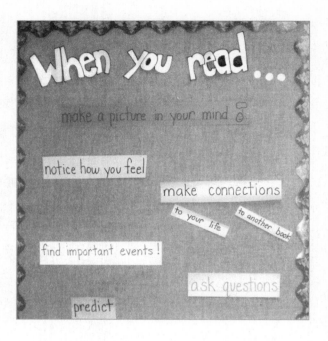

53 Genres

Post this handy, informative chart near your class library. To create, make a list of book genres, using a different-colored marker to identify each one—for example, write "Fiction" with an orange marker, "Science" with a green marker, and so on. Beside each genre, draw a dot of the same color. Then place colored dots on the inside cover of each class library book according to its genre. You can also place a bit of masking tape on the spine of each book and use markers to dot the tape.

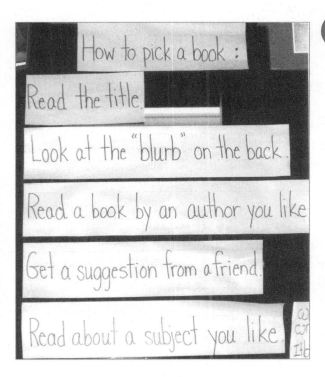

54 How to Pick a Book

This chart offers strategies to help students find a book that's just right. Write guidelines on sentence strips and post them on this chart. Children can refer to the chart when picking books to read independently. Use the strategies offered here, or provide your own.

Terrific Tip: Recording guidelines on alternating colored strips makes this chart easier for children to read.

55 Ways We Choose Books

Brainstorm with students a list of reasons they choose the books they do. There are no right or wrong answers for this chart; sometimes a cover catches our eye, sometimes a friend recommends a book, and sometimes the illustrations look cool. See how many ways students report they choose books—then add some of your own for them to consider, including your own favorite method for testing readability levels.

Ways We Choose Books
- Like the genre D.C.
- Like the author A.O.
- Heard from a friend T.K.
- Read other books in series A.H.
- Already read, read aloud L.J.
- Interested in cover D.C.
- Interested in hobby-book about that hobby A.N.
- Title that sparks interest K.J.
- Liked the summary on back A.P.
- Great illustrations H.A.
- Saw the movie N.K.
- Interesting words A.C.
- Book on my level T.R.

56 Why Readers Abandon Books

This chart, a companion to the Ways We Choose Books chart, invites students to share reasons why they stop reading a book they've chosen. It allows students to abandon recreational "reads" without feeling that somehow they have failed as a reader, and it reminds them to never judge a book by its cover.

Terrific Tip: Have students sign their initials to each contribution—a great way to help students "own" their own learning.

Why Readers Abandon Books
- Boring—not interesting T.K.
- Not funny N.C. / Too funny T.K.
- Too hard A.C.
- Too Easy D.C. T.R. M.W.
- Decided this series is not for you A.N.
- Not crazy about genre T.R.
- Disappointing sequel N.K.
- Not what you expected V.M.
- Can't "get lost in story" K.T
- Illustrations don't go with story A.N
- Can't relate to characters A.N.
- Don't like what's happening in story A.N.
- Book is too confusing A.C.

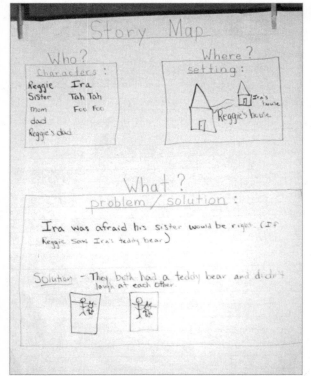

57 Story Map Question Box

Get at the heart of stories with this chart. By answering three basic questions—Who? Where? and What?—students will automatically provide information about characters, settings, and problems/solutions.

Terrific Tip: To help expand the information on this chart, have students answer additional questions, such as Why? (motive), When? (time), and How? (method).

58 Story Map List

This handy chart lists story elements in the simplest terms possible.

> **Terrific Tip:** Copy this chart onto 8 ½" x 11" paper. After each element, provide a blank line for writing. Reproduce a supply of these fill-in-the-blank mini-charts, and have students complete one for each book or story they read. Use mini-charts as discussion springboards. Store completed mini-charts in folders meant just for this purpose. That way students have a record of what they've read all year long.

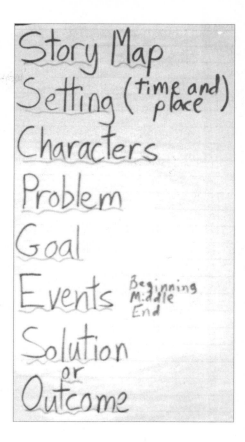

59 Reading Responses

This chart cites the various aspects of a book—from author to style—and then poses questions related to each for the reader to reflect on as he or she reads the book. These questions are great to review before and after children engage in recreational reading. You can also choose one question a day for children to ponder and/or write about. The questions can be reproduced on 8 ½" x 11" paper and given to students to tape to the inside cover of their Reading Response Journals.

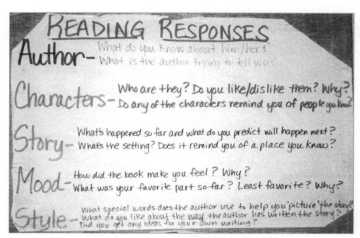

60 Components of a Book Review

This chart for older students offers several sophisticated elements students can weave into their book reports or reviews. The ideas go beyond having students simply tell whether or not they liked a book, including persuasive "sales" techniques designed to encourage audience members to read the book too.

Components of a Book Review

1. Attracts the reader's attention with a great first sentence.

2. Gives a brief description of the book (highlights interesting parts).

3. Leaves the reader hanging. (Inspires the reader to read the book.)

4. Tells the title and author of the book.

5. Tells who the book is appropriate for (grade level/age, language, interest).

6. Gives your opinion about the book.

61 Rules for Literature Circles

Here's a great example of how a well-crafted teacher-made chart can help students become self-directing. With clear, simple language, children can see at a glance who is responsible for the tasks at hand.

Literature Circles

Discussion Director - controls the group, leads

Summarizer - explain what has happened

Literary Luminary - good, interesting parts and words.

Connector - explain how the book is like something else.

Vocabulary Enricher - look up new or interesting words

Illustrator - draw a picture

Terrific Tip: The jobs on this chart are listed in the order they'll most likely come up in the group. While there will be some back and forth among the roles, this basic organization offers students a sound structure and direction for getting started.

Pumpkin Jack

Author: Will Hubbell

Beginning: Tim had a pumpkin and he made it into a Jack O-Lantern.

Middle: It started to rot. He put it in a garden that had dead flowers. The pumpkin became flat and the seeds went into the ground. Tim found a little plant. The plant grew into a pumpkin.

End: He carved another pumpkin and named him Jack, too.

62 Beginning, Middle, Ending

Help beginning readers divide a story into three main parts with this simple yet powerful chart. In addition to noting the beginnings, middles, and endings of stories, experienced readers can also be asked to cite story conflicts, climaxes, and resolutions.

63 Book Buddy Reading

Use this chart to list and define the different labels you use to describe shared-reading experiences in your classroom. The chart shown here lists Choral Reading, Chunk Reading, Echo Reading, and Role Reading, but your chart will reflect the labels you use.

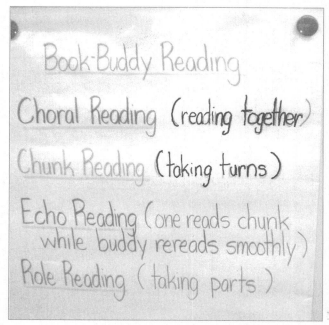

Book-Buddy Reading

Choral Reading (reading together)

Chunk Reading (taking turns)

Echo Reading (one reads chunk while buddy rereads smoothly)

Role Reading (taking parts)

64 Literary Genres

This straightforward chart lists and defines ten different literary genres. Your chart can feature more or fewer genres, depending on your class's needs and abilities.

Terrific Tip: You can "grow" this chart over time by initially listing only a few genres and adding additional ones as the year goes on.

Genres

Realistic Fiction - A made up story, that could happen.

Nonfiction - Factual information

Biography - a person who writes about someone else.

Autobiography - a person who writes about them self.

Fairy Tales- Make believe, not true.

Science Fiction - A made up story that has some science or technology tied in.

Historical Fiction - A made up story with some historical facts.

Poetry - Words in verse, with feeling, may rhyme.

Plays - Stories that are broken into scenes and parts.

Folk tales - Stories, passed down, from different countries

65 Components of a Biography

Create a concise list of the components of a biography and share with students. The chart shown here was created on a computer, so it's clear and easy to read. It's also short enough for students to remember.

Components of a Biography

1. Includes significant aspects of the person's whole life.

2. Contains detailed description or dialogue which reveals the person's personality.

3. The information included is carefully researched and true.

4. Documentation is available for further research.

Elements of a BIOGRAPHY

- If the person is DEAD or ALIVE and when they died.

- When and where they were born.

- Quotes from the person who the biography is about.

- The education of the person.
- Sometimes they include a timeline.
- Things the person accomplished.
- The personality of the person.
- Any difficulties they faced growing up.

- Why they are famous.

- Tells about their family.
- Tells what talents they have. (Hobbies etc.)
- What they wanted to be when they grew up. (To be compared to what they actually did become.)
- Who the person's role models are, who they admired.
- Any illnesses.

66 Elements of a Biography

This chart contains a student-generated list brainstormed in class. It contains more detail than the teacher-generated chart above, and it offers students a fuller framework for creating their own biographical writing.

67 Characters List

How many characters have your students met in their reading travels? Create this elegant, simple, and powerful chart by listing characters that students have known and loved. Remember to use contrasting colors, so the names are easy to read.

Terrific Tip: Create a companion chart of corresponding questions (e.g., *Who is your favorite book character and why? What character reminds you of you? Which character would you most like to be like?*) and use it as a springboard for discussion or a writing prompt.

Characters

Jack	Sharon	Robert
Annie	Andrew Marcus	Goomy Bud
Junie B. Jones	Nicky Lane	Patty Jane
Horrible Harry	Miss Kelly	Theodore
Ping	Hegedy Peg	Halloweener
the Emperor	Henry	Arnie
Chrysanthemum	Mudge	Lord Mouth George
Lily	Miss Nelson	Philip
Amos	Miss Viola Swamp Frog	
Boris	Rainbow Fish	Toad
Doug	Ira	Harriet
Song Lee	Reggie	
Miss Mackle	Bertie	
Sidney	Eloise	

68 Rate Your Book

Now students can use a star-studded rating system to tell whether or not they liked a particular book. This chart shows them how to rate a book using one to five stars.

Terrific Tip: As a companion display, create a Student Star Ratings Chart. Write a book title at the top of a sheet of chart paper, and list student names underneath, down the left-hand side. Students can then use star stickers, a star-shaped stamp, or hand-drawn stars to post their ratings for the book, along with their names. This should prompt a lively book discussion as students explain why they rated a book the way they did.

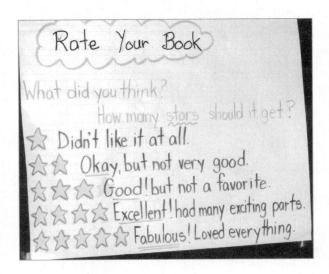

69 Hula Hoop Venn Diagram

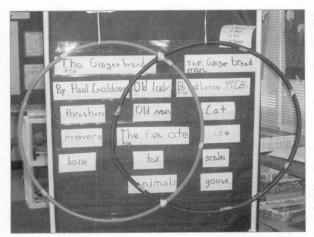

To create this eye-catching and unique display, use masking tape to join two Hula Hoops together so they overlap, as in a Venn diagram. Then use string to hang the overlapping hoops from the top of a pocket chart stand. Give students sentence strips so they can record and display elements unique to each item being compared (two stories, characters, settings, etc.) in the spaces to the left and right. In the overlapping space in the middle, they can display the elements the two items have in common.

70 Character Mitten

Create a collaborative-writing chart based on your reading of the classic tale *The Mitten* as retold by Jan Brett. Use craft paper to cut out a large mitten shape and attach small line drawings of the various story characters. Then have children create name tags for the characters, which you can add to the chart.

71 Rebus Rhyme

Just the addition of some small, simple drawings turns this ordinary seasonal poetry chart into a rebus chart with key words illustrated. When trying this rebus technique with your own classroom charts, have students suggest words to be illustrated, or try underlining words you want them to take turns illustrating.

72 Tips for Reading Aloud

This unique chart helps children become aware of how punctuation and text formatting (such as the use of italics) can change the way text "sounds" even when read silently. This awareness can also help children apply these techniques when adding emphasis to their own writing.

When do good readers change their voice?

all capital letters - louder
question mark - up
exclamation points - excited
quotation marks - character
speech bubbles - character
letters are different font - bent

73 Storybook Castle

This charming fairy-tale castle chart is the perfect place to "house" story parts. The one shown here features turrets and towers with plenty of room for the title, main characters, time, place, problem, and solution. Consider adding glitter glue to make your castle really sparkle. Fun to build, and a most memorable place for children to visit and revisit.

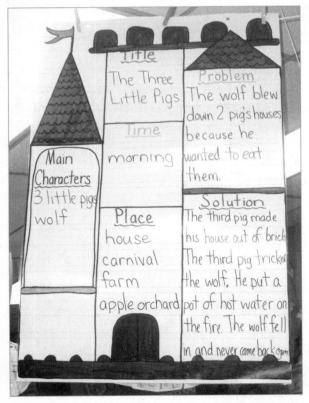

74 What Do We Notice About Fairy Tales?

Create this chart as a way to get students to think and talk about the characteristics of fairy tales. Before creating the chart, show students a sampling of fairy tales they're already familiar with. Have them review these books to help them recount the story elements in these tales. Record these on your chart and add to the list over time.

What do we notice about fairy tales?
- animals talk and wear clothes.
- hair can grow long to have someone climb it.   · magic   · witches
- princes   · princesses   · talking silverware
- fairies   · flying   · giants
- Once upon a time   · Happily ever after

75 Making Connections

This chart helps students relate text to self. Divide a piece of oaktag or craft paper in half vertically. On the left side, print the subtitle "When I read the part about . . ." and on the right side, print the subtitle "It reminded me of . . ." Then choose a story detail or event, or let children choose, and print it on the left side of the chart. Have children take turns telling what this detail or event reminded them of in their own lives. Record these connections in the right-hand column. Remind students that good readers are aware of how the events in the stories they read connect with the events in their own lives.

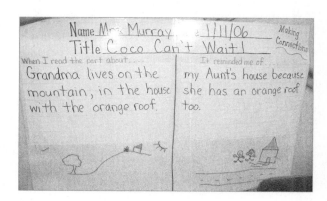

76 What is Your Favorite Reading Memory?

To create this chart, first print the question, "What is Your Favorite Reading Memory?" and add a simple shade tree to set the mood. Then, talk with students to help them recall the people and places from favorite reading memories. Use different-colored markers to record each memory, and write them as prepositional phrases ("with Grandpa," as opposed to just "Grandpa"). Use this chart to prompt a writing assignment about the special people and places children associate with reading.

77 I Wonder . . .

This simple but powerful chart is perfect for use with reading or writing activities. At the top of the chart print the words "I Wonder . . ." followed by the five Ws and H: Who? What? When? Where? Why? and How? Remind children to be on the lookout for answers to these questions as they read, and to provide answers to these questions when they write.

Good Writers:

1. make their pictures match their words.
2. have good details in their pictures.
3. have an uppercase letter at the beginning of each sentence.
4. use mostly lowercase letters.
5. use spaces between words.

78 Writing Tips

Invite students to use collaborative thinking and discussion along with cooperative writing to help create this simple chart that lists the qualities of a "good writer." Because children are the ones defining what a good writer is, in terms they understand, this chart holds meaning and invites additional contributions as students learn more.

Terrific Tip: Have students develop companion charts defining good students, good teachers, good schools, good friends, and so on.

79 A Good Writer . . .

Help children define what you mean when you refer to a "good writer." Use the ideas shown here or provide your own.

Terrific Tip: Add one quality at a time so children can work on their writing with that element in mind.

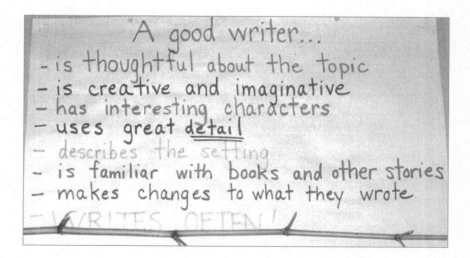

A good writer...
- is thoughtful about the topic
- is creative and imaginative
- has interesting characters
- uses great detail
- describes the setting
- is familiar with books and other stories
- makes changes to what they wrote
- WRITES OFTEN!

80 I Don't Know What to Write About

This simple chart addresses a common lament that most teachers are familiar with. It offers children four simple ways to spark thoughts about writing topics. Feel free to add your own ideas to inspire students' writing.

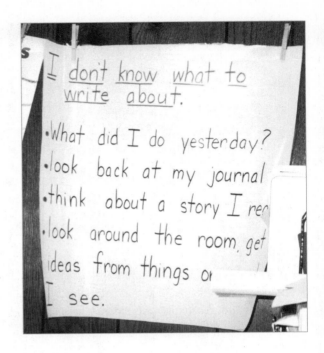

I don't know what to write about.

• What did I do yesterday?
• look back at my journal
• think about a story I rea
• look around the room, get
  ideas from things or
  I see.

Topics I can write about.
1. Nana or Pop-pop
2. My friend _____
3. Write about my favorite toy
4. Going to the hospital
5. Holidays
6. Favorite animals
7. Pets
8. Trip to : ice cream store
             a pet store
             vacation

81 Topics I Can Write About

Here's another way to solve the "What should I write about?" dilemma. Have children generate a list of writing topics from their own experience (e.g., family, friends, toys, illnesses, pets, trips, memories, and so on). They can refer to this list whenever they feel they've run out of ideas.

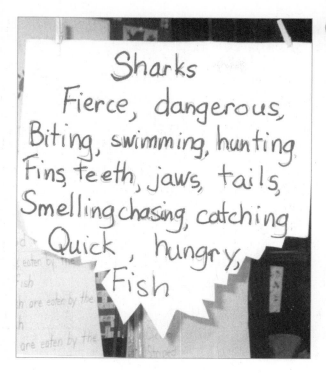

82 Shark Words

Have children brainstorm a list of words that remind them of sharks. Print these words in random fashion on a piece of chart paper. Then add visual appeal by cutting gashes in the bottom of the paper—as if a shark had really swum past and taken a bite or two out of the chart! When read together, the individual shark words sound poetic.

83 Writing Web

Use chart paper to help kids spin a web of writing ideas. In the chart shown here, students brainstormed different ideas, facts, and topics related to dolphins, but you can use this web with any topic or theme. As you begin to chart ideas, more writing possibilities automatically emerge.

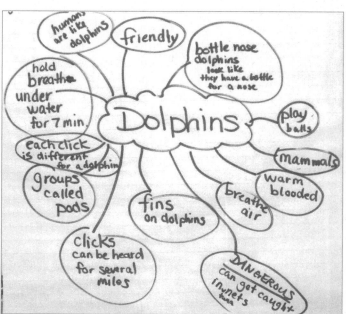

84 Write What You Know About, Care About, Worry About, Wonder About, Like, Love, and Hate

When it comes to what to write about, this chart says it all. It fuels ideas for writing by inviting children to connect their thoughts with emotions. You can have students brainstorm as you record their responses directly on the chart or use a separate sheet of paper to list children's ideas.

Write what you know about
                     care about
                     worry about
Pets, dogs, cats, hamsters   wonder about
When I got lost   like
little brother   love
beanie babies   hate
holidays
Something you can't wait for

a trip you've been on   vacations

birthday
family — aunts, uncles, cousins, grandparents
        mom, dad, brother, sister or pets 🙂

make a story out of something that
has happened!

85 Imperfect Pairs

List some compelling superlatives on chart paper and use them to spark creative writing responses. On the chart here, the teacher listed 12 superlatives and then chose one—"the smallest"—to pair with common objects. The whimsical pairings work as an automatic creative writing springboard: as children attempt to picture the possibilities, stories practically write themselves!

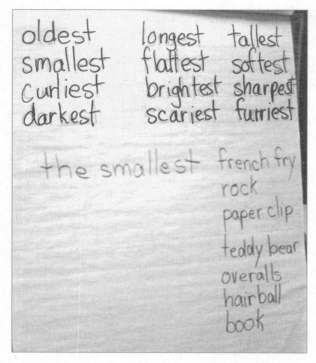

oldest   longest   tallest
smallest flattest softest
curliest brightest sharpest
darkest   scariest furriest

the smallest   french fry
               rock
               paper clip
               teddy bear
               overalls
               hairball
               book

Things	we can write about.	
People	Places	Things
aunt	the city	dolls
mom	store	book
dad	McDonalds	mittens
grandpa	school	toy
uncle	Chuckie Cheese	gum
grandma	carnival	clothes
(pet)	zoo	car
brother	China	
cousin	Disney World	
sister	Splish Splash	
best friend	beach	
teacher	Arizona	
	Florida	

86 Things We Can Write About

This chart offers students clear ideas for writing topics based on familiar specific nouns. To make, divide a piece of chart paper into three vertical columns. Title the entire chart "Things We Can Write About." Then label the columns "People," "Places," and "Things," using a different color for each. Solicit examples of each type of noun from students and record their ideas in the appropriate color. Remind students to refer to the chart when thinking of topics to write about.

87 Writing Small Moments

Help your students understand that good writing doesn't have to be about the really huge events but can also center on the small, quiet, everyday moments we all share. This chart offers a simple method your students can try as they work to recount the details of small moments: *Think of pictures in their minds, sketch out the pictures, write the words.*

Writing Small Moments
1. Writers think about something that happened to them.
2. They think of the picture in their mind.
3. They sketch out the picture.
4. They write the words.

Terrific Tip: Help students understand that the act of "sketching out the picture" can mean to actually sketch an illustration, or it can mean to "sketch" the picture in their imaginations.

88 How to Write a "Friendly" Letter

Use a colored marker to write a letter on chart paper. Then use a marker in a contrasting color to note formatting details, such as where to indent and where to skip lines. You can also use this same technique to highlight parts of a letter, such as the date, salutation, body, close, and signature.

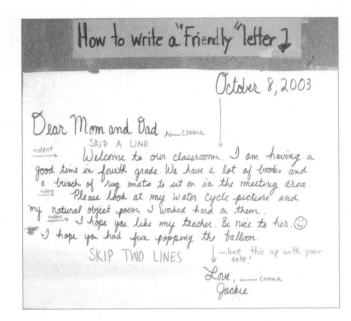

89 How to Address an Envelope

Draw an oversized envelope on chart paper, then address the envelope, including a return address as well. Draw a stamp on the top right-hand corner. Have children refer to this model when addressing "real" mail.

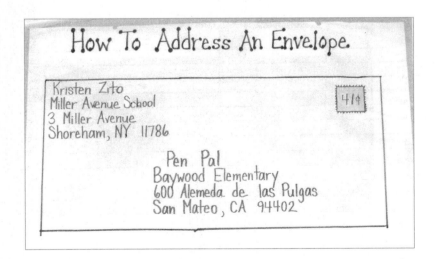

What Can We Write About A Book?

- Tell about the illustration
  - What made them good
- Tell about any interesting word
- Was it a good title? Why?
- Tell about a connection?
- What did you learn?

90 What Can We Write About a Book?

This chart is perfect for beginning readers and writers who are being asked for the first time to write in response to a book. Note that the first question on the chart invites children to respond to the book's illustrations. Illustrations help support the text and are easier for some children to notice and remember when responding.

> **Terrific Tip:** The phrase "Tell about a connection" invites the child to either connect text-to-self or text-to-text— whatever connection pops up first.

91 When You Write, Remember That . . .

To create this chart, write the following sentence starter on a sentence strip: When you write, remember that . . . Then on separate sheets of chart paper, list qualities of good writing that you want your students to remember and employ. Be sure to phrase them so they complete the sentence starter. You can then rotate the various reminders, using magnetic spring clips to display them.

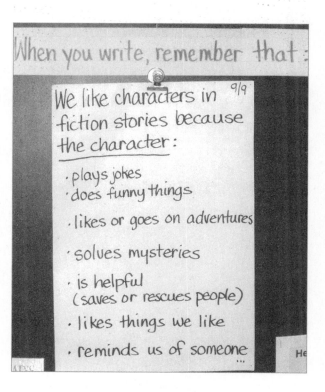

When you write, remember that :

We like characters in 9/9
fiction stories because
the character:

- plays jokes
- does funny things
- likes or goes on adventures
- solves mysteries
- is helpful
  (saves or rescues people)
- likes things we like
- reminds us of someone
  ...

92 What Is a Poem?

Do your students really understand what a poem is? Do they think poems have to rhyme or follow a particular pattern? This chart helps define the attributes of a poem. Use the qualities shown here, or add some of your own.

Terrific Tip: After creating and/or sharing this chart with your class, why not share a few poems aloud to see if they each fit some, most, or all of the criteria?

A Poem :
* Can be about anything
* Can use few words
* May or may not have rhyme
* Ends with a punch
* Has a title
* Lets us know the poet
* Is easy to create

93 Worn-Out Words Chart

This simple but clever chart reminds students that "worn-out words" are like "worn-out jeans"—comfortable, but overused. Record worn-out words on paper pieces that resemble patches. The chart also suggests that students use *synonyms* to give those worn-out words a break!

Terrific Tip: Additional patches labeled with worn-out words can be added over time.

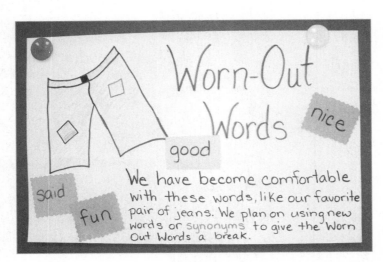

Worn-Out Words

good

nice

said

fun

We have become comfortable with these words, like our favorite pair of jeans. We plan on using new words or synonyms to give the Worn Out Words a break.

94 No Overused Words

This chart sends the message that some overused words are off-limits. Choose four or five words that students overuse, print them on a chart, circle the words, and draw a red slash across the circle. Over time you can replace this chart with a new set of overused words.

95 In Place of "Said"

Do your children overuse the word *said* when they write? This clever chart lists a whopping 54 words students can use instead of *said*. Can you think of more ways for your students to introduce dialogue?

> **Terrific Tip:** Remember, writing in alternating colors makes the chart more readable.

In Place of "Said"

- say
- cried
- demanded
- boasted
- exploded
- thundered
- explained
- replied
- advised
- stammered
- bragged
- whispered
- agreed
- gestured
- screamed
- inquired
- murmured
- sighed

- exclaimed
- confessed
- continued
- added
- shouted
- gloated
- giggled
- asked
- breathed
- answered
- retorted
- gasped
- snapped
- yelled
- called
- boomed
- announced
- begged
- scolded
- repeated

- echoed
- barked
- suggested
- questioned
- quoted
- reminded
- began
- spoke
- creaked
- stuttered
- ordered
- laughed
- whined
- complained
- insisted
- stated

96 What's Another Word For . . . ?

This interactive mini-chart collection invites students to offer synonyms for overused words.

> **Terrific Tip:** Place the sheets of paper and a marker in a learning center so children can add to the lists when inspiration strikes.

97 From Ordinary to Extraordinary

Show students how to transform their overused words into powerful ones that make their writing "pop"! To do this, divide a piece of chart paper in half vertically. Label the left-hand side of the chart "Ordinary" and the right-hand side "Extraordinary." List ordinary words on the left (e.g., *nice, good, bad*) and the extraordinary equivalents on the right (e.g., *agreeable, fantastic, terrible*).

> **Terrific Tip:** Provide several extraordinary words so children's writing will have variety.

UNFORGIVABLES!

a	big	go	into	now	so
about	but	going	is	of	some
after	by	got	it	off	that
all	came	had	just	on	the
am	can	has	like	one	their
an	come	have	little	only	them
and	could	he	look	or	then
are	day	her	made	our	there
as	did	here	make	out	they
at	do	him	me	over	this
back	down	his	more	said	to
be	first	I	my	saw	two
because	for	if	no	see	up
been	from	in	not	she	very

was went when who would
we were where will you
well what which with your

98 Unforgivables!

It is unforgivable for kids to struggle to spell common sight words. This spelling chart will really come in handy when children are writing. It lists alphabetically all the frequently used words children should know how to spell.

Terrific Tips: To make this resource easier for children to read, use a different-colored marker for each set of words beginning with the same letter. This is also a great chart to reproduce for children to keep in their reading or writing folders.

99 When to Use Capitals

A straightforward chart showing how we use capital letters in writing. If students make errors in capitalization, you can simply refer them to this chart; they can then begin to self-edit and see for themselves how and why their work was not correct.

Terrific Tip: You can create similar charts addressing other issues of grammar and mechanics, such as punctuation use, subject-verb agreement, rules for creating plurals, and so on.

CAPITALS

1. I
2. Holidays
3. Months
4. Starting sentences
5. Titles of stories, poems, books
6. Days of the week
7. Names of people
8. States
9. Countries
10. Places
11. Cities, Capitals
12. Continents
13. Planets
14. Excitement
15. Starting of a quote
16. Dear in a letter

All About Nouns

This chart is a variation of the "Things We Can Write About" chart (page 55). It draws attention to the different types of nouns, and invites students to use collaborative writing to record examples of each.

Terrific Tips: Include one sentence that contains all three types of nouns—person, place, and thing—in order, as in "The <u>boy</u> went to the <u>park</u> on his <u>bike</u>. You might also allow space to explore and record proper nouns.

Noun Person, Place, Thing

Person: Miss D   Brian
Susan Mom   Brother Sister

Place: Ridgeshcool   classroom
Store   Movie theater
Chuck E. Chease

Thing: Video Games   pen
Candy Pocketbook Headband
Book Dragon

The boy went to the park on his bike.

Proper Nouns: Need Capitals!

 Adjectives Are Describing Words

This chart tells what an adjective is and gives examples. First write a clear definition of *adjectives*. Then invite students to tell you the adjectives they know, and use collaborative writing to record them on the chart. Note that contrasting-colored markers help raise the readability factor.

Adjectives
are
Describing Words

Words that tell about something and add detail to writing

Bumpy ordinary
lumpy   sloppy
pink silly   old   gleaming
scary Very Smart fluffy
Yellow Smooth
tiny Normal Grumpy
pretty terrible
horrifies
Big

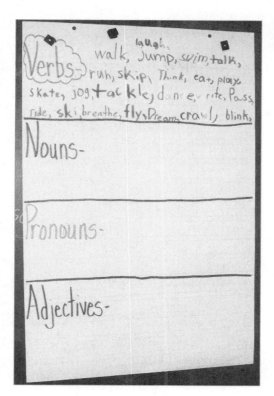

102 Parts of Speech

This chart is one you can set up and complete over time as students learn the different parts of speech. To make, simply divide a sheet of chart paper into four equal spaces. Label the spaces with the four major parts of speech: *Nouns, Verbs, Pronouns,* and *Adjectives.* Then, as students bring their focus to each of these word types, they can provide examples.

> **Terrific Tip:** Make similar charts to display other parts of speech: Adverbs, Conjunctions, Articles, and so on.

103 Strong Verbs and Nouns

What are Strong Verbs? They're verbs that don't need a lot of adverbs. What are Strong Nouns? They're nouns that don't need a lot of adjectives. Provide students with blank word cards and encourage them to harvest strong verbs and nouns from literature and poetry and add them to your chart.

> **Terrific Tip:** Make companion charts featuring Cool Adjectives and Spicy Adverbs.

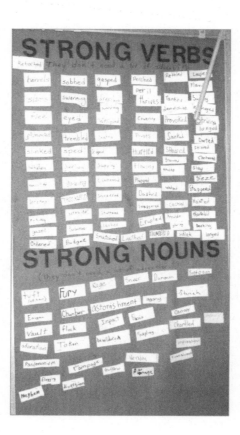

104 Homophones Chart

This helpful chart tells what a homophone is and provides examples. You can develop the chart further by providing sentences using the different homophones.

> **Terrific Tip:** This same format can be used to present any number of word types and parts of speech, such as synonyms, antonyms, compound words, conjunctions, and articles.

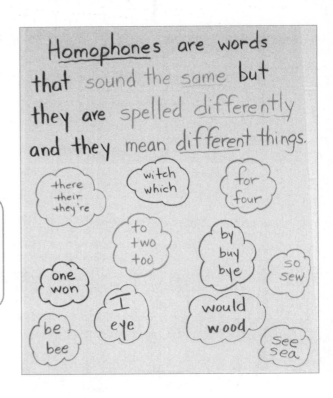

105 What Do I Do When I Can't Spell a Word?

This chart offers children ideas to try when they cannot spell a word. Your chart can include the ideas shown here and/or other ideas, such as *Look at the word wall, Write it two different ways and see which one looks correct, Sound it out, Check my spelling folder, Ask a neighbor or teacher, Take my best shot and wait and check it later.*

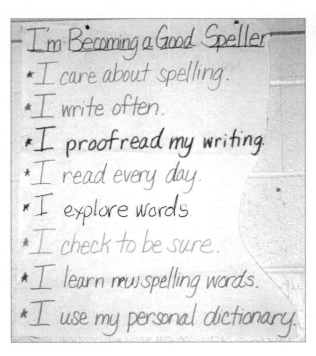

 ## 106 I'm Becoming a Good Speller

Offer children evidence that they are indeed learning to spell well. This chart points out the many ways children's spelling is improving as they put their ever-widening skills to use.

> **Terrific Tip:** Make similar charts to let children know they are growing in other areas, such as reading, math, behavior, and so on.

 ## 107 5 Steps for Great Illustrations

This clever chart offers students five steps to creating illustrations that support text. You can use the steps shown here, or create five of your own.

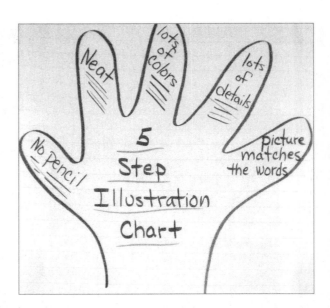

> **Terrific Tip:** Placing any information into a five-step plan makes the information easy for students to remember.

108 When Writers Illustrate They . . .

Here, five separate but interrelated charts tell students how to develop an illustration from start to finish. Directions include: *Sketch*, *Outline*, *Color*, *Go Back*, and *Add Details*. Altogether, the illustrations nicely demonstrate the progression from sketch to finished product.

Ways to end our writing

As you can see

Clearly

That is why

Finally

In my opinion

Personally I think

Now you can see

In conclusion

In closing

109 Ways to End Our Writing

Sometimes the same students who have no trouble beginning to write don't know how to effectively *stop* writing! This chart offers students a list of phrases for bringing writing to a close. Many of the phrases work equally well for fiction and nonfiction. This is a chart your students will really appreciate and use.

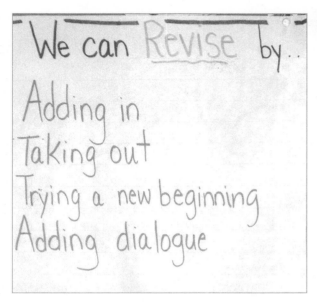

We Can Revise By . . .

It's often wise to revise, but do your students really understand how to revise without totally rewriting their work? This chart lists four simple but powerful techniques students can use when revising.

> **Terrific Tip:** After students try one of these suggestions, have them take turns reading the original and revised versions aloud to see if classmates think the revisions they incorporated actually improved their writing.

111

Workshop Rules

This chart of workshop rules helps students self-navigate through independent workshop sessions when you are busy conferencing with other students. The chart will ensure children know what to do if they get stuck.

> **Terrific Tip:** From time to time, review the steps on the chart, so they become second nature to your students.

Workshop Rules
(Reading & Writing)

- Always do your best
- If you're stuck, try to solve the problem yourself then ask a friend.
- Never interrupt a conference.
- If you really need to ask me a question slip me a post-it.
- Go on to something else while you're waiting

112 Peer Conference Tips

This chart offers four clear and easy steps young children can follow to support each other during a peer conference. Of course, free to adapt the chart so it fits the procedures children follow in your classroom.

> Peer Conference...
> 1. Give your partner a topic.
> 2. Help your partner add on.
> 3. Give your partner a compliment.
> 4. Listen to your partner read their work.

> If you want to conference:
> ① Did you do your revisions?
> ② Did you edit your work?
> ③ Did you read to a partner?
> ④ Did you let a partner read your story to you?
> Is this a piece you want to publish?
> Sign Up for a publishing conference

113 If You Want to Conference

This chart is great for helping students slow down enough to realize if they are truly ready for that all-important Publishing Conference with you. The chart features a four-step review process students must pass through (self-revision, self-editing, peer conferencing, and peer-reading) before they answer the big question: *Is this a piece you want to publish?* Provide room at the bottom of the chart for "serious" writers to sign up.

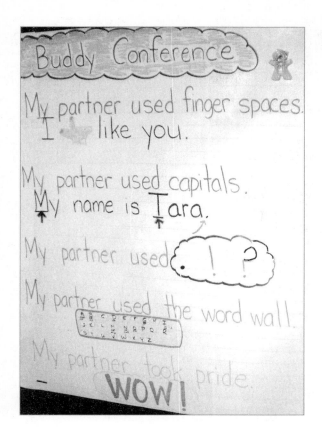

114 Buddy Conference Tips

Here's a checklist younger children can refer to when learning how to support a classmate's writing efforts. Provide a sample to illustrate each of the five conferencing points.

> **Terrific Tip:** Transfer this chart to a piece of copier paper, and then place a supply of these checklists in your writing center. When conferencing, children can use the checklists to review and then "sign off on" their buddy's work.

115 What to Do Before Publishing a Book

Children love writing books, but in their haste to get "published" they can sometimes overlook details in the editing process. This chart can help children make sure their book is ready to go.

> **Terrific Tip:** Make individual copies of this checklist chart and place in students' notebooks or writing folders.

What to do before publishing a book
* Reread
* check for capitals and lowercase letters
* check spelling by circling unknown words
* go back to add more descriptions and details
* check for: . ?!
* read with a buddy
* make sure it's your best work

116 How Do I Know When I Am Done?

This checklist chart helps children to ensure that everything in their work has been checked and corrected. The last item on this list—"I took pride in my work"—suggests that they, not you, know when they have really done their best.

> **Terrific Tip:** Notice that the chart above is very clear and easy to read. Neatness does count—especially when it comes to the teacher's handwriting!

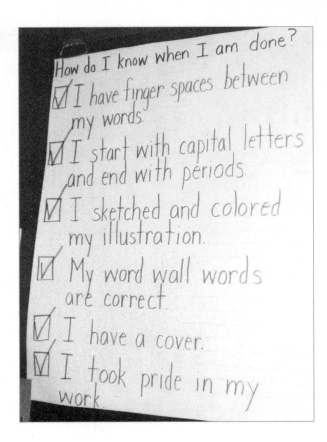

How do I know when I am done?
☑ I have finger spaces between my words.
☑ I start with capital letters and end with periods.
☑ I sketched and colored my illustration.
☑ My word wall words are correct.
☑ I have a cover.
☑ I took pride in my work.

117 What Do I Do When I'm Done?

This very basic chart is a good one for beginning writers. It reminds children to check that they have added punctuation, written their name and date, and have read the piece to a classmate. Adapt the chart as you wish, but keep it simple.

What do I do when "I'm done"?
• make sure you remembered a period., a question mark? or an exclamation point!
• put your name on your paper
• stamp the date on your paper
• read it to a classmate

118 3-D Pattern Block

Use real wooden pattern blocks to create this simple but effective chart. List the names of the shapes on a piece of oaktag, laminate the oaktag, then use packing tape to attach the blocks to the chart, as shown.

> **Terrific Tip:** Position a tub of blocks beneath the chart as shown here. As children build and work with the blocks, they can simply glance at the chart to see the correct name for each shape.

119 Paper-Doll Class Graph

Give each child a simple paper doll and some art supplies and invite children to decorate their dolls to look like themselves. Then create a graph by drawing a numbered grid on a sheet of chart paper and displaying one doll in each section of the grid. Title the display "How Many Girls? How Many Boys?"

120 Number Board

Round stickers from the office-supply store and a piece of oaktag are all you need to make this number chart, which shows the quantitative geometric relationship among amounts ranging from 0 to 10. You can use dots of the same color, as in the chart shown here, or different-colored dots on different rows.

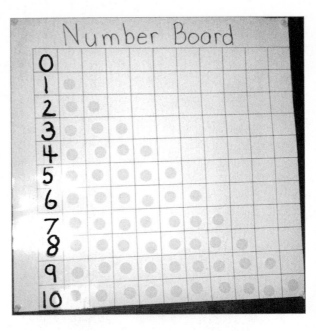

121 Odd and Even

To make this chart, divide a sheet of chart paper down the middle and label one side "Even" and the other side "Odd." Then write the even and odd numbers on the appropriate side of the chart, from 1 to 20. Beside each number, invite students to provide a visual representation of the number by tracing square sticky notes and then coloring them in. Notice that the teacher who created the chart here included the words *partners* and *leftovers* to distinguish even quantities from odd.

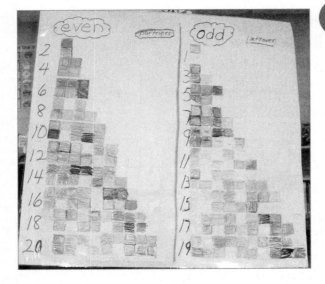

122 Question of the Day

This simple graphing chart invites children to use spring-type clothespins (printed with their names) to answer a daily yes-or-no question. Magnetic clips hold the top of the chart to a magnetic board. This way, the chart itself hangs free so children can easily slip the clips onto the chart. Number each horizontal line from 1 to 20, beginning at the bottom of the centerline and moving to the top.

123 Class Survey

This Yes/No chart is a great first interactive chart for young children. Instead of posing a question, it offers a simple choice (e.g., laces/no laces) and a simple choice of responses ("Yes! Yes! Yes!" or "No! No! No!"). To place their responses, children use wooden spring-type clothespins labeled with their names and decorated with markers.

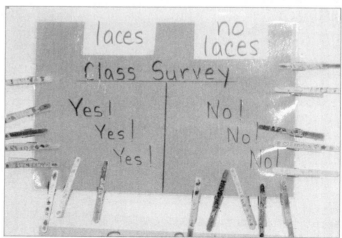

124 ## Yes/No Pocket Chart

In this version of the Yes/No graph, use a pocket chart and index name cards to have children answer yes or no to a question posted above the chart.

> **Terrific Tip:** Keep this chart fresh by changing the question daily or weekly.

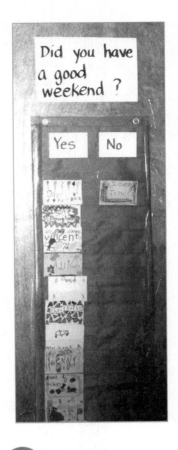

125 ## Favorite Flavor

This fun-filled chart is made from three paper ice cream cones and "scoops" of popular flavors. First, label the paper cones with three flavors and attach them to the bottom of the chart. Then pass out one paper circle per child and ask children to color the "scoop" so it resembles their favorite flavor among the three choices. Have children place their scoop on the corresponding cone. When all the students have added their scoops, count them up and note the number of each flavor. Which flavor is the most popular? The least?

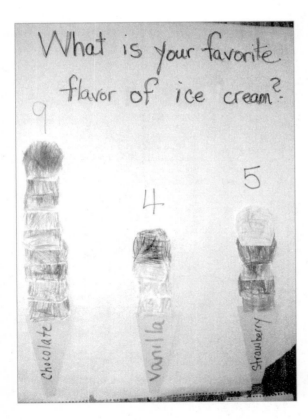

126 Favorite Colors

This interactive chart uses colorful sticky notes to create a graph of favorite colors. Children each choose a sticky note that matches their favorite color and then print their name on that note. The notes are then added to the chart (with same-color notes stacked together in columns) to create an instant graph. Add color labels along the bottom of the chart and a tissue paper rainbow at the top to complete the display.

127 Monthly Weather Graph

These graph designs are perfect for younger children. Create columns on grid paper to note four different types of weather (sun, clouds, rain, and snow). Then each day, color in one space on the grid to track that day's weather. Make a new chart for each month and compare results from month to month.

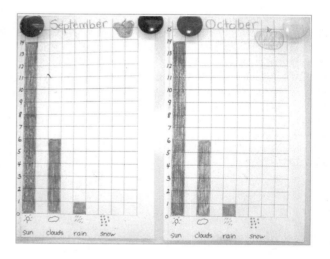

Terrific Tip: Leave a blank column between each graphed column, so the chart is easy for children to read.

128 Counting Candy Wrappers

This chart puts candy wrappers to good use. Ask children to bring in candy wrappers from home (shortly after Halloween is the best time). Then work with children to sort the wrappers alphabetically and glue them onto ABC charts. Finally, have children count the number of wrappers that begin with each letter and note those numbers on the charts.

129 Pet Graph

To make this chart, use markers to divide a piece of chart paper into a grid with enough columns to represent the number of pets your students have at home. Then have children enter their names (this chart used removable name strips, so the chart is reusable) under any and all categories of pets they own.

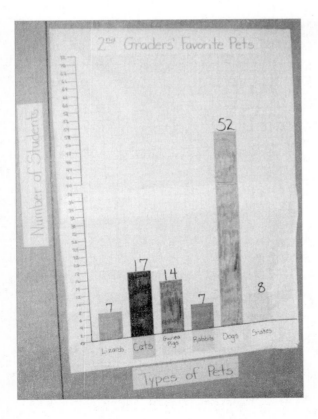

Terrific Tip: You can also use the same chart model to create a separate companion chart titled "Pets We Wish We Owned." Compare the two charts to see how many children already own the pets of their dreams!

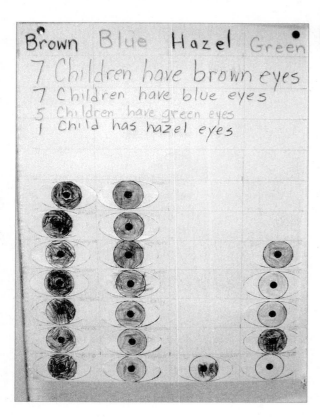

Brown Blue Hazel Green
7 Children have brown eyes
7 Children have blue eyes
5 Children have green eyes
1 Child has hazel eyes

130 Eye Color Graph

This eye-catching chart lets you graph students' eye color. First, create and cut out paper "eyes" and hand out one per child. Ask children to color their eye so it's the same color as their own eyes. Then create columns for each eye color in your class and have children add their eyes to the chart. Finally count up the number of each color and note this on the chart.

> **Terrific Tip:** Older students may want to create similar graphs of their family members' eye colors.

131 Hair Color Graph

To create this chart, you'll need yarn in shades of brown, black, yellow, and red. Have each child select a piece of yarn (or a combination of colors) that most resembles the color of his or her hair. Tie the yarn pieces into bow shapes and have children place their "hair" directly onto the grid. This chart features blonde, dirty blonde, brown, black, and red, but you may want to include other hair colors such as strawberry blonde, light and dark brown, and black.

> **Terrific Tip:** Have each child sign his or her name to the appropriate yarn sample.

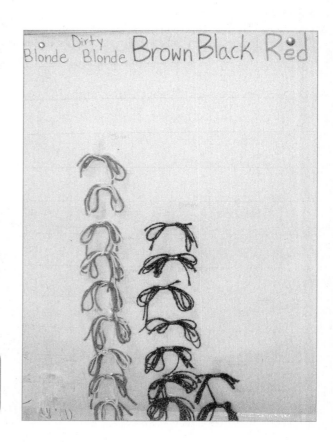

Blonde Dirty Blonde Brown Black Red

132 How Many Letters Are in Your Name? (Version #1)

Personalized charts really capture children's attention. This name chart has students graph the number of letters in their own names. Use grid paper to create a graph, as shown here, with numbers running from 1 to 15 along the bottom. Write children's names down the left-hand side of the graph. Have children shade in the appropriate number of spaces to chart the number of letters in their names.

Terrific Tip: Use alternating colors to make the chart more readable.

133 How Many Letters Are in Your Name? (Version #2)

For this chart, have children build their first names from commercial alphabet letters and glue them onto colorful construction paper to create "nameplates." Then help students sort their nameplates according to the number of letters in each name.

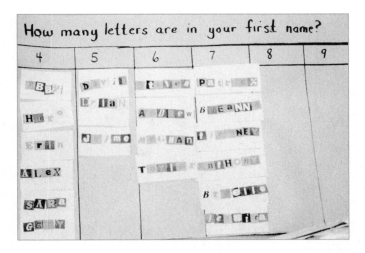

134 Name Mini-Charts

These mini-charts provide another way to group names based on their number of letters. Here, individual charts contain names with four, five, or six letters (you may need more than six). By grouping names on individual charts and building the names from same-sized letter blocks, students can clearly see the one-to-one correspondence of the different letters in the names.

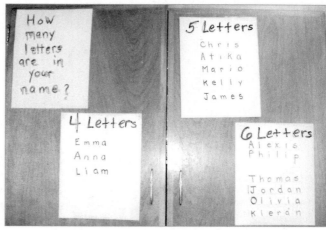

135 Pet Tally

What pets do your students love? Create this chart to find out. The chart uses tally marks to record students' favorites. With this chart model, children may cast a vote for an animal whether or not they have that animal for a pet.

136 100th Day Tally

Use tally marks to count the first 100 days of school. The children who created this chart had so much fun they didn't want to stop when they reached 100. They used blue tally marks (seen under the dividing line) to count the remaining days of the school year.

137 Monthly Tally Charts

Have your students count their way, month by month, to the 100th day of school. Together, count the school days in each month, and mark them on the chart. Then count each set of tally marks to find the total number of school days in each month. On the 100th day, add all the tallied sums to see if the grand sum equals 100.

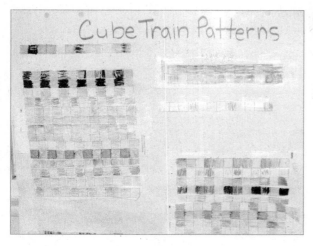

138 Cube Train Patterns

The children who worked to create the pattern train chart shown here, first created patterns using 12 plastic linking cubes. They then used crayons to transfer the same patterns onto graph paper and displayed the results together on a large piece of chart paper.

Terrific Tip: After children create this chart, challenge them to take turns using the cubes to build each other's cube trains as displayed.

139 How to Make a Pattern

To make this chart, brainstorm with children different ways we can show patterns, and then provide an illustration of each. This chart illustrates patterning by color, shape, size, and other creative ways. Use the patterns shown here, or come up with some of your own.

Terrific Tip: Revisit this open-ended chart so it grows over time.

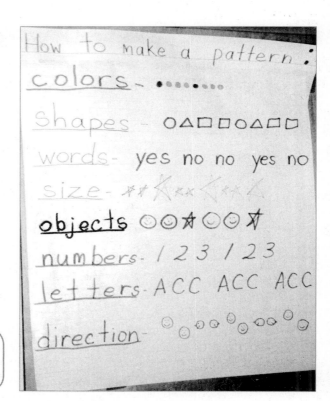

140 Sticky-Note Clock

Turn your classroom clock into a teaching timepiece! Simply place small sticky notes numbered by fives at each numeral. Students can see how to skip-count the minutes in an hour by five.

Terrific Tip: Use the papers to label the numbers on the right side of the clock face (from 12 to 6) with the numbers 5 to 30, and the numbers on the left side of the clock face (from 6 to 12) the same way. This way you can demonstrate to children why we use particular language to refer to the minutes *until* or *before* the next hour (e.g., "It's ten minutes before 5.").

141 Write-On, Wipe-Off Clock

Here's a chart that fits over your classroom clock face. It shows children the digital minutes from 00 to 55, with hour spaces left blank so you and students can fill them in, depending on the position of the hour hand. You can simply laminate the chart and fill in spaces with a dry erase marker.

Terrific Tip: Add a note reminding children that the short hand is the hour hand and the long hand is the minute hand.

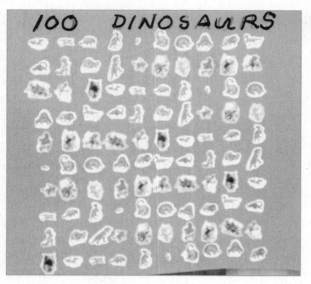

 142 ## 100 Dinosaurs

A first-grade student created this wonderful chart to celebrate the 100th day of school. To create similar charts, your students can decorate oaktag with a collection of 100 items such as stickers (of any theme or design), thumbprints, rubber-stamp images, recycled stamps, stick figures, and so on.

 143 ## My 100 Words

This student-created chart is similar to the dinosaur chart above, but this one features an alphabetized display of 100 words cut from magazines and newspaper flyers.

Terrific Tip: For a challenge, students can collect 100 words beginning with the same letter, or 100 words connected to a particular theme.

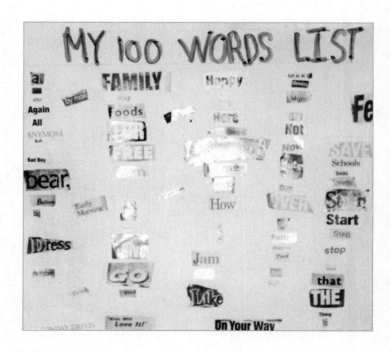

144 100 Crayons

Divide 100 new (or gently used) crayons into sets of 20. Use clear packing tape to attach the crayons to a piece of chart paper as shown here. Then use a marker to draw a line above each row of crayons and between each crayon in the row. Number each crayon from top to bottom, 1 to 100.

Terrific Tip: Create another colorful chart by using 100 different crayons. On a sheet of chart paper, use each crayon to make a list of all 100 color names.

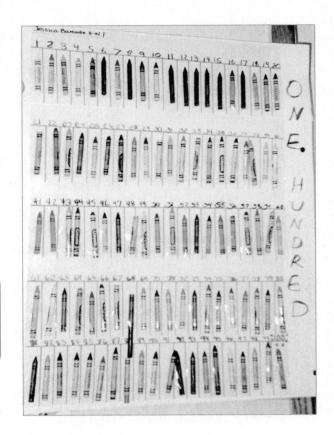

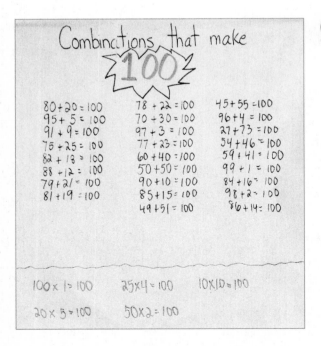

145 Combinations That Make 100

How many number combinations can your students think of that add up to 100? How many multiplication sentences can they think of that result in a product of 100? Create this chart with your students to find out.

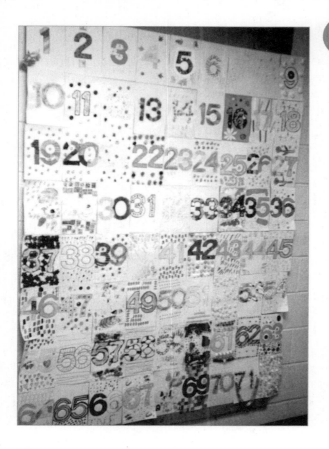

146 Decorated Numbers

Trace large bulletin board numerals onto drawing paper to create mini-posters of the numbers 1 to 100. Then invite children to use art supplies to decorate the posters. The number of decorations used on each poster must match the number being decorated. For example, if a child decorates the number 33, he or she may place 33 dots (or stickers, pompoms, hearts, stripes, stars, and so on) in and around the number. When all the numbers have been decorated, arrange the posters in order from 1 to 100, to create a large class chart.

147 Ways to Show $1.00

Play money (or real coins) can be used to make this chart that neatly and clearly displays and compares coin amounts (pennies, nickels, dimes, and quarters) equaling one dollar. Just place coins down on a piece of oaktag and cover with clear adhesive paper. Priceless.

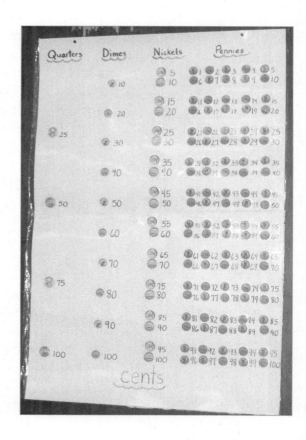

148 We Can Count by Fives

Here's a handprint chart your students can really count on—by high-fives! Create an "ink pad" using a large sponge coated with a bit of finger paint. Then have students work together to press their hands on the sponge and then onto the paper to create this handy counting chart.

Terrific Tip: You can create this chart in a single day, or over time by having students take turns adding a handprint for every five days of the school year.

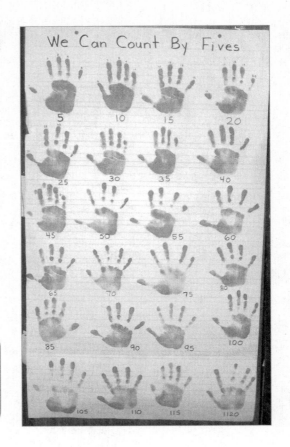

149 Fraction Chart

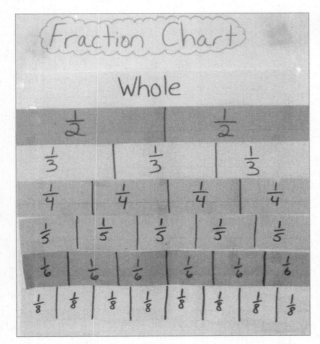

Colorful sentence strips serve as the basis for a fascinating fraction chart. To make this chart, fix seven sentence strips in contrasting colors (e.g., yellow, orange, green, blue, pink) onto a piece of oaktag or plain chart paper. Label the top sentence strip "Whole" and then divide the remaining strips into segments representing halves, thirds, fourths, fifths, sixths, and eighths. Students can easily count and compare the different numbers and sizes of fractional segments that equal one whole.

150 Ways to Add

How many different tools can children use to add numbers?
This chart lists seven. Can your class think up more?

Terrific Tip: Use this same chart model to have children brainstorm a list titled "Ways We Use Numbers in Our World."

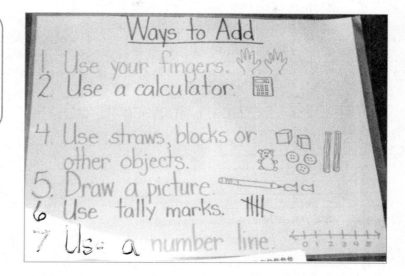

151 Words That Tell Us to Add

Here's a chart that helps students become aware of key words that signal a particular math operation—in this case, addition. When students are able to "decode" such word problems, they gain mastery over math and the mystery is solved.

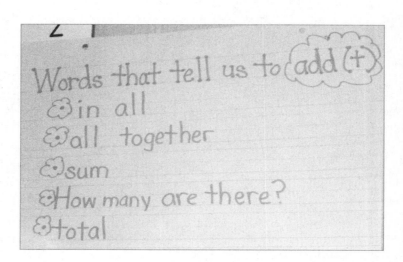

152 ## Subtraction Words

This simple chart focuses on words that signal subtraction and displays your children's growing math vocabulary. This is a helpful chart for children to refer to when journaling their math questions, explanations, or solutions.

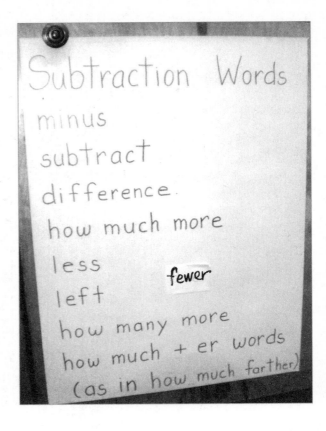

153 ## Addition and Subtraction Tips

This clever chart offers a collection of vocabulary belonging to two separate math operations: addition and subtraction. Print the words on sentence strip segments and attach them to craft paper.

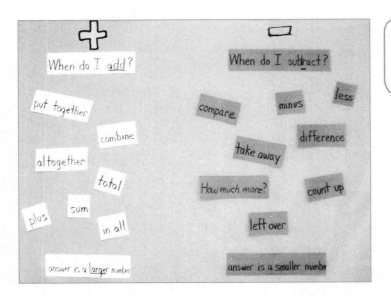

Terrific Tip: Be sure to use different colors so the two operations are distinct.

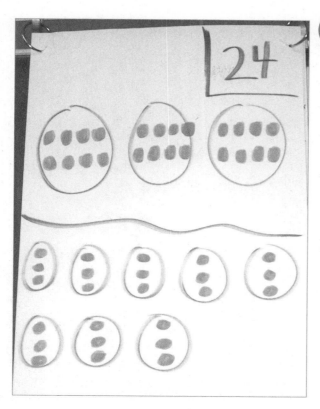

154 Ways to Group 24

The number 24 can be made in a number of different ways. It can be made with three sets of eight or eight sets of three, for example. This handy flip chart invites children to explore all the ways to make 24. It also demonstrates how multiplication and division are related operations.

155 Multiplication Chart

To make this chart, cut paper squares in different colors and use them to represent sets of numbers. The paper squares shown here represent sets of four. The chart also includes labels showing the relationship between sets and multiplication.

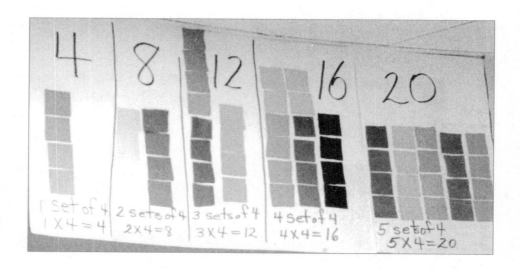

156 ## Multiples of . . .

Each of these charts features multiples of a particular number.
As you can see, the multiples are listed in a random fashion
on the chart.

> **Terrific Tip:** Record the
> multiples in different colors
> to ensure the chart is easy to
> read.

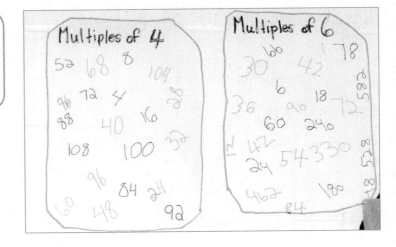

157 ## Place Value

To make this chart, divide a piece of craft paper into three
segments or periods (ones, thousands, millions), and print
a large comma at the base of each column. Then print three
numerals in each section and use the space above each numeral
to label each one's place, from ones to hundred millions.
Challenge children to read the number from left to right.

> **Terrific Tip:** To
> change the number, print
> other numerals on craft
> paper segments and
> tape over the original
> numerals.

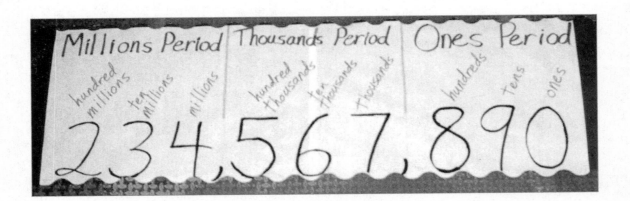

> Underline
> Look next door
> Five or more
> Add one more

158 Rounding Numbers Up

This catchy rhyme gives children the steps to rounding numbers up. First, students underline the numeral in the place they wish to round off. Then they look at the number to the right to see if it's five or more. If it is, they round up by adding one to the underlined number and changing the number on the right to zero (e.g., 46 rounds up to 50).

159 Rounding Off

Viewing this chart, students will easily grasp the idea of what it means to round off numbers to the nearest ten. To make the chart, draw and label a curved line as shown here. Use the chart to show students that if the digit in the ones place is five or more, they round up the number in the tens place, and the digit in the ones place becomes zero. If the digit is less than five, they reduce the digit in the ones place to zero, and the digit in the tens place stays the same. For example, 57 is rounded up to 60, and 53 is rounded down to 50.

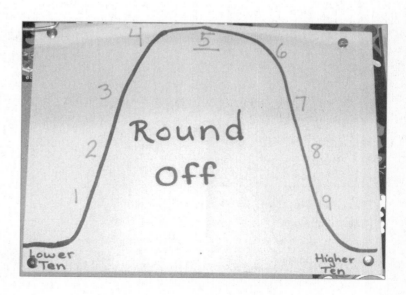

160 Word-Problem Strategies

Here's a chart for helping younger children tackle math word problems. It lists five simple problem-solving steps they can follow. The process of reading through these steps invites children to think up other solutions of their own.

> **Word Problem Strategies**
>
> 1. Reread the problem
> 2. Draw a Picture
> 3. Work Backwards
> 4. Guess & Check
> 5. Ask a friend

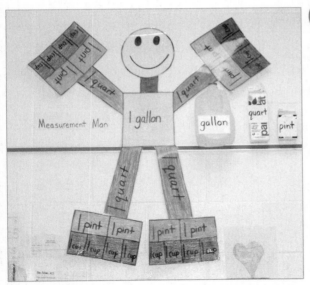

161 Measurement Man

How many cups are in one pint? How many pints are in one quart? How many quarts are in one gallon? Measurement Man can easily answer these liquid quantity questions. Explain to students that quantities that are adjacent to (i.e., that touch) another larger quantity are equal to that larger quantity. For example, two cups touch one pint, and four quarts touch one gallon.

Terrific Tip: Consider making an alternate "Measurement Madame" to show other relative amounts, such as whole and fractional teaspoons and tablespoons.

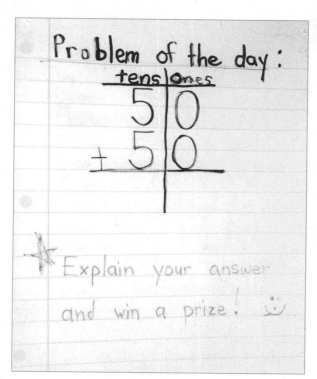

Problem of the Day

Print a math problem on a piece of chart paper. Invite children to solve the problem and to explain their answers in writing. Provide children with math journals for this purpose. Meet with children at a regular time each day to discuss solutions. Print these below the problem. Circle the solutions everyone agrees on (and that you know are correct). Each day, print a new problem on a fresh sheet of paper.

163

How Did We Count Big Numbers?

Divide your class into small groups and offer each group a large number of objects to count. Challenge each group to find a way to calculate the number of objects in its collection. Have each group share its strategy. Record these on the chart.

> **Terrific Tip:** Use this same chart model to have children report their problem-solving approaches to other math challenges, as well as other challenges across the curriculum.

How did we count big numbers?

Table 1. Keith, Brendan and Michael N. counted by ones - they got 432, they got confused so the number is not really correct.

Table 2: Michael L. counted by ones, Joe counted by tens.

Table 3: They made piles of tens. = 391

Table 4: They counted by ones. Kyle made piles of 50!

Table 5: Made bunches of tens. They got 235.

164 Math Mini-Charts

These four simple charts define four important math terms that students need to know: *sum, difference, product,* and *quotient.* Use different-colored paper for each term. Then provide a number sentence that exemplifies each one.

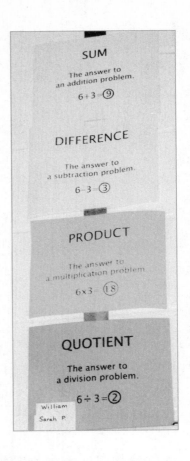

165 Problem-Solving Strategies

This chart, aimed at older children, offers a number of ways to solve math problems successfully. Creative solutions include acting the problem out and using logical reasoning. The many offerings here appeal to any number of learning styles. Feel free to add your own ideas.

> **Terrific Tip:** Because children have different problem-solving preferences, don't number the items on the chart. Instead, allow children to pick and choose the strategies that appeal to them.

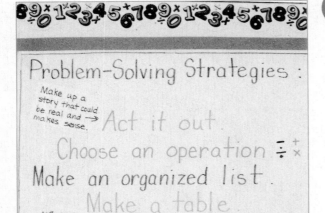

166 Weather Words Chart

Help your students keep track of the weather. This catchy little chart has room for students to display more than one weather condition at a time. It's easy for students to change weather labels throughout the day as the weather changes.

167 Weather Watch

This chart helps students observe the weather and analyze their findings. To make the chart, use several rubber stamps of simple weather images (clouds, sun, a flag flapping to represent wind, and so on) to mark several pads of square sticky notes. Then, on a sheet of chart paper, display sentence strips that pose questions and statements about the weather. Each day, children can place one or more notes in the appropriate category. Encourage them to compare and analyze their findings. How does September's weather compare to October's?

168 Our Favorite Seasons

This charming graph chart is a snap to create with chart paper and sticky notes. After discussing seasonal memories with the class, offer students sticky notes and invite them to draw an image that reminds them of their favorite season. Divide a sheet of chart paper into four horizontal spaces large enough to accommodate the sticky notes. Label each horizontal space with the name of one of the seasons. Then have children place their notes to indicate their preferences and to create an instant seasonal graph.

169 Five Senses

To make this chart, divide a piece of blank paper into five relatively even sections. Label each section with one of the five senses along with an icon to represent each sense. Have students brainstorm words related to all five senses.

170 Our Favorite Apples

Create this chart after an apple-picking field trip — or simply bring in some varieties for your students to taste and compare. To create the chart, divide a piece of lined chart paper into columns. Along the bottom, write the names of the apple varieties, with pictures, if possible. Then allow children to write their names in a space above their favorite. Leave space between the columns so chart is easier for children to use and read.

171 Color Words

Here's an easy idea for making color charts for beginning readers. First, select a color to focus on and provide a marker in that color. Have students use collaborative writing to record items of that color. (For example on the chart here, students used a green marker to list green things such as grapes, grass, frogs, and so on.) Invite students to take turns illustrating each item on the list.

172 Who Lost a Tooth?

This chart asks the all-important tooth question, and then answers it very clearly.

Terrific Tip: You may want to make your display larger than this one. Notice that only two months into the school year, this chart is filled to the brim with paper teeth.

173 Apple Investigation

Do all apples have the same number of seeds? This interactive chart lets you use the simple four-step scientific method (question, prediction, experiment, and conclusion) to find out. Follow the steps and record your findings.

Terrific Tip: Have students use collaborative writing to pose the question on your chart.

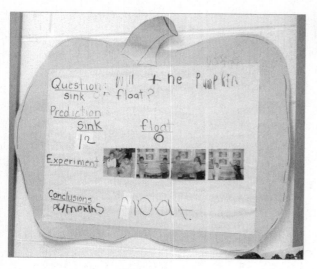

174 Pumpkin Prediction

Will a pumpkin sink or float? As with the Apple Investigation Chart, this chart helps you use the scientific method (question, prediction, experiment, and conclusion) to find out.

> **Terrific Tip:** Use this chart model to conduct other investigations with the class.

175 Cool Clouds

Use a digital camera to capture color photos of cloud varieties to create this beautiful chart. Print the photos and mount them on a large piece of craft paper. Then label the type of each cloud as well as the date the photo was taken.

> **Terrific Tip:** You can also find similar full-color photos of cloud types on the Internet. Simply download and print.

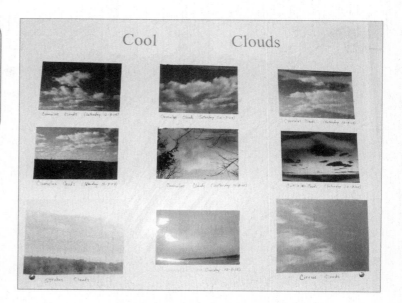

176 Types of Clouds

This chart offers students labeled line drawings of three basic cloud types (cumulus, stratus, and cirrus). Leave room for students to add words to describe each one.

Terrific Tip: Use cloud photos as shown in Cloud Chart #1 (above) to enrich this chart.

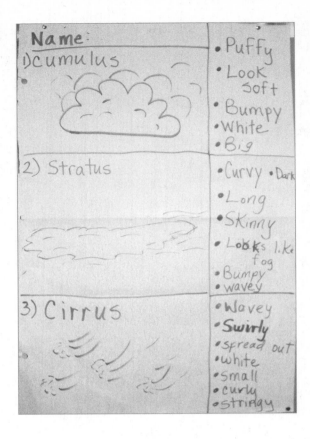

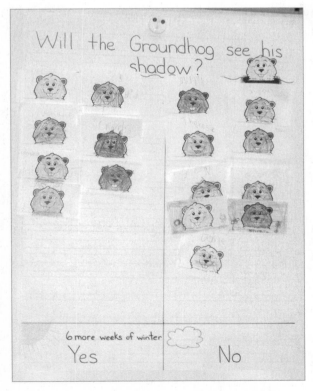

177 Will the Groundhog See its Shadow?

This fun-filled graph chart asks children to predict whether the groundhog will see its shadow on Groundhog Day. Give each student a groundhog face to color. Then have children place their groundhog on either side of a simple yes/no T-Chart. Help children place the faces in neat columns so they can easily compare the number of responses.

Tree Comparison

Help students learn about different types of trees with this chart, which compares two common species. The chart clearly and effectively compares the shapes and sizes of the same plant parts (the stem, the leafstalk, the blade) as they appear on the two different trees. The chart can be expanded over time to include other tree varieties common to your area.

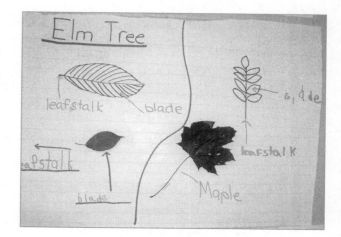

Properties Word Chart

This chart explores five common properties of matter: color, shape, texture, size, and weight. Use the chart to help students notice physical attributes that help describe and define a person, place, or thing. The chart can also serve as a springboard for considering other, more sophisticated attributes, such as body covering (fur, feathers), height, width, hue, and so on.

180 Dino-meter

This chart organizes information related to different types of dinosaurs. To make, divide a sheet of chart paper into five columns. Use the first column to list a series of questions related to dinosaurs (e.g., *What is its name? What did it eat? Did it walk on two legs or four?* and so on). In the remaining four columns, answer the questions.

Dino-meter				
What was its name?	Stegosaurus	Triceratops	Brontosaurus	Tyrannosaurus rex
What did it eat?	Plants	PLANTS	Plants	Meat
Did it walk on 2 legs or 4?	4	4	4	2
Did it have a long neck?	No	No	Yes	No
How long was it?	20ft	30	85	40
What did its footprint look like?				

181 Bat Parts

Go "batty" with this chart, which uses students' collaborative writing to label a bat's body parts.

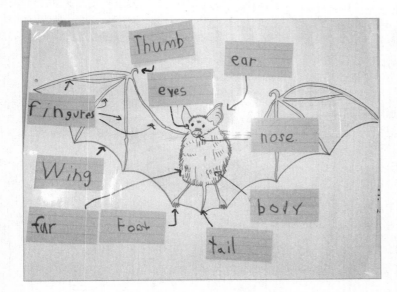

Terrific Tips: Use this chart model to help children develop vocabulary associated with other themes or topics as well. You might invite older students to create detailed drawings related to one theme or topic (animals, machines, toys, landforms, book characters, the skeleton, buildings, and so on) and then have your students use collaborative writing to create labels that turn the drawings into detailed, informative diagrams.

182 Stay Active Collage

Celebrate physical activity with this collage constructed from
an assortment of photographs of students and pictures cut
from magazines.

Terrific Tip:
Students can use
this display as a
springboard for
writing exercises and
personal narratives.

183 What Do We Know About Leaves?

This chart lists information children know to be true about leaves. In
the model shown here, target sight words are underlined, illustrating
how you can use one chart for a variety of lessons.

Terrific Tips: This is a wonderful
chart to use at the beginning of a
thematic study, because it helps
you determine children's current
understanding of the topic you're
about to explore. If, through
subsequent study, you discover that
any statement on the chart isn't true,
draw a line through it and add the
new understanding to the bottom of
the chart. Additional information can
be added over time.

What do we know about leaves?
1. Leaves fall from trees.
2. Leaves are all different colors.
3. Leaves have stems.
4. Leaves grow on trees.
5. Leaves change color in the fall.
6. Leaves have points.
7. Leaves have different shapes.
8. Leaves are nature.
9. Leaves can be collected.
10. Leaves can be raked into a pile.
11. Leaves can be thrown up into the air.
12. Leaves can be used as decorations when they dry up.

184 Venn Diagram

A Venn diagram is an excellent chart for helping children organize and understand the interrelatedness of information they're exploring. This one works well because it's color coded, with yellow on the right, blue on the left, and a green space in the middle where the two circles overlap. Labels above the diagram coordinate with the circles and the shared center space.

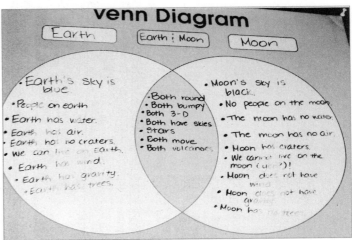

185 Words We Know In Sign Language

This chart features a list of words children have mastered. This particular chart lists sign language words, but you can make charts of thematic words or words that contain a particular phonetic feature or spelling pattern.

Terrific Tip: Using different-colored markers to create the list makes it easier for children to visually attend to a particular word or words on the chart.

What You Learn From A Label

1. How much <u>sodium</u> (salt) the food has in it
2. How much <u>fat</u> the food has in it
3. How much <u>protein</u> the food has in it
4. The <u>ingredients</u> used to make the food
5. How many <u>servings</u> are in the package
6. How much is in a serving
7. How many <u>calories</u> are in a serving
   Calories mean how much energy the food gives us
8. How much <u>calcium</u> we get from a serving
9. What <u>vitamins</u> are in the food.
10. If it's good for us

186 What You Learn From a Label

For an accessible, real-life reading experience, you can't beat a food label. This chart notes nine pieces of information that appear on packaged-food labels. Children can refer to this chart when comparing information offered on different food labels.

> **Terrific Tip:** Define some or all of the unfamiliar vocabulary present on the labels.

187 Tooth Fairy Letter

Here's a wonderful way to offer children a fun and authentic experience with correspondence. Begin by reading some books about the Tooth Fairy, and then talking with students about what questions they would ask the Tooth Fairy if they could. Help students use collaborative writing to incorporate their questions into a chart-size letter to the Tooth Fairy. Then, on a separate sheet of chart paper, compose a response from the Tooth Fairy.

March 2, 2006

Dear boys and girls,
   Thank you for your letter. Yes, you are all on my list. You will all lose your teeth. Just be patient and keep taking care of them. Brush them at least twice a day, eat good healthy food, and I will be visiting while you sleep. Goodluck in first grade! See you soon!

Love,
The Tooth Fairy

Fact and Opinion

Students often have difficulty differentiating between fact and opinion. This chart helps clear things up. First, the chart defines both terms, and then it offers several student-generated examples of each.

Terrific Tip: To strengthen and clarify this chart, be sure to color code each term, it's definition, and the corresponding examples.

Fact and Opinion

Fact – Something absolutely true
– Can be proven

Opinion – What you think
– How you feel

Facts: Cheetahs can run 70 mph.
Sharks eat fish
We go to Ridge School.

Opinions: Miss D is the best teacher.
School is fun.
Math is cool.

189 **Story Development**

Divide a piece of chart paper into six boxes. Make the first three boxes smaller than the last three. In the first box, begin telling a story. In the second box, reiterate the first part of the story and add details and phrases to it. In the third and fourth boxes, continue adding to the original sentence. Then, in the fifth box, introduce a new character who asks for clarification about the story events. Use the final box to answer this question by recounting and reiterating the entire list of story details.

Terrific Tip: This chart model can also be used to help retell plots from books and stories children have read.

> Some ways to use notebooks
> • Questions or things you wonder about.
> • Memories, Feelings, Dreams
> • Quotes, Interviews Opinions
> • Images that stick out in your mind
> • Eavesdropping - overheard conversations
> • Family stories
> • "Talking to yourself" on paper
> • Responding to literature
> • Plans for a project

190 Some Ways to Use Notebooks

This chart lists a number of ways children can use writing notebooks or journals. It's the perfect chart to refer children to when they simply can't think of anything to write about. Get creative and add some ideas of your own.

191 Words Used to Add Information

This chart is great to post near the science center or wherever you store students' science notebooks. The chart offers students a list of words and phrases to use when they want to add information: *again, also, and, besides, another, next, for example, for instance, finally, as well as,* and *along with.*

> Words used to add information
> "again" "also" "and"
> "besides" "another" "next"
> "for example" "for instance"
> "finally" "as well as"
> "along with"

192 **Words Used to Compare**

This chart highlights words and phrases students can use in their writing to compare people, places, and things: *in the same way, similarly, as, like, likewise,* and *also.* When children use these words their writing will flow.

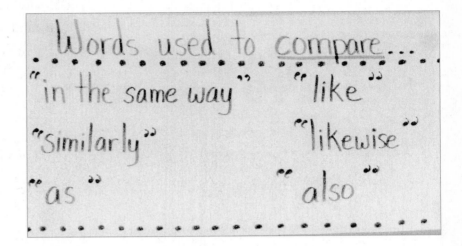

193 **Words Used to Contrast or to Show Differences**

This chart lists words and phrases students can use in their writing to cite contrasts or differences between things or ideas: *but, on the other hand, yet, otherwise, however, still, although, even though,* and *rather than.* These words help show the relationships between things and ideas and help make meaning clear.

(194) Words Used to Conclude

Now you can offer students a chart full of words and phrases that help them wind up their writing: *as a result, finally, therefore, lastly, in conclusion, in summary,* and *in short.* Remind children that variety is the spice of good writing.

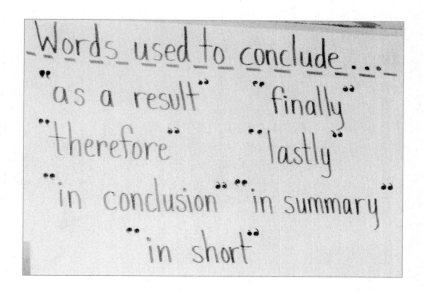

(195) Computer Words

Here's a chart to help students become computer literate so they can work more independently. It presents a word wall of computer terms that children should get to know. Introduce these one at a time as the need arises, then review periodically to make certain children understand the definitions and how they apply to their computer literacy.

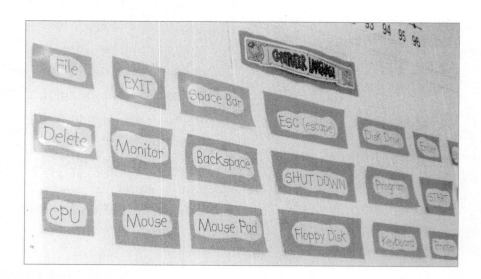

196 Wishes

Generate a large list of fantasy wishes children can consult when stuck for a writing topic. Every so often invite children to expand the list to keep it fresh and exciting.

> **Terrific Tip:** Harvest playful "what if" ideas from experience, TV, dreams, movies, and literature. For example, *What if you owned a big red dog?*

Wishes

- twelve moms
- a quad
- $1,000,000
- a genie
- $1,000 (to find it)
- X-Box
- race/sports CAR
- Lord of the Rings – Game Cube
- a treasure
- to be rich
- a puppy
- dogs
- fairy god parents
- a castle
- 200 pieces of gold
- a Playstation II
- 10 cows
- wife
- century's stock of candy
- a cat
- to own an ice skating rink
- to be fancy
- to be on t.v.
- to drive
- to be an artist
- to work with animals

197 Kind Words

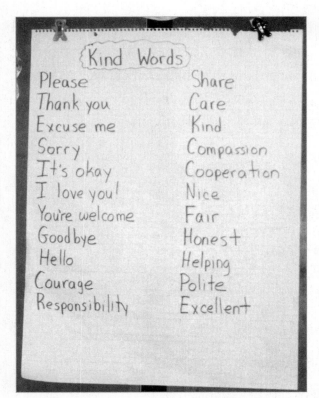

This chart reminds students that kind and caring words are important—and it offers a whole collection of kind words students (and teachers!) can incorporate into their speech to raise the kindness level in the classroom. Get the ball rolling by printing the words *Please* and *Thank you* at the top of the list. Then invite students to offer additional words for the chart. Challenge students to add more kind words as they arise in their conversations and experiences, or in the literature they read. Can students list 100 different kind and caring words?

Kind Words

Please	Share
Thank you	Care
Excuse me	Kind
Sorry	Compassion
It's okay	Cooperation
I love you!	Nice
You're welcome	Fair
Goodbye	Honest
Hello	Helping
Courage	Polite
Responsibility	Excellent

HOW TO DRAW A BUTTERFLY

① Draw a small circle.

② Draw a long oval.

③ Draw two circles.

④ Draw two smaller circles.

⑤ Draw two lines with dots.

⑥ Add details!

198 How to Draw a Butterfly

Teach children the importance of following directions with this step-by-step butterfly chart. Post it on your wall and invite students to complete this quick art project as a treat for finishing their school work.

199 A Friend Is . . .

Even emerging writers can use this list-poem chart to easily generate a lengthy poem. Begin each line of the poem with the same two words, "A friend . . ." and have children take turns completing the line. At first, children will likely contribute simple adjectives (e.g., kind, good, nice). But if shown how, they will begin to add descriptive phrases (e.g., "Someone who comes to your house," "Someone who helps you tie your shoe").

A Friend is . . .

A friend is kind.
A friend is super.
A friend is nice.
A friend is good.
A friend likes me.
A friend helps you.
A friend plays with you.
A friend takes you to the nurse.
A friend picks flowers for you.
A friend says nice things to you.
A friend shares snack.
A friend helps you up when you fall down.
A friend makes you cards when you are sick.
A friend picks you for the bookpet.
A friend helps you tie your shoe.
A friend is awesome.
A friend is great.
A friend invites you to a birthday party.
A friend comes to your house.
A friend doesn't say mean things to you.
A friend doesn't laugh at you when you make a mistake.
A friend laughs with you.
A friend can sleep over.
A friend reads with you.
A friend is super-duper.
A friend is special.

200 ## A Year to Remember

Display photographs from your year together. Display the photos however you wish, in chronological order or in collage form. The chart works beautifully as a prompt for a discussion or a written "scrapbook" page to help children remember and celebrate all the learning and growing that took place throughout the year.

201 ## Scrapbook Wall

Turn one or more classroom walls into an expandable scrapbook. Invite students to contribute photos from home and to supply poems and memoirs to accompany the pictures.

Terrific Tip: Create a living "School Days Scrapbook" by posting photos and corresponding writings of classroom events throughout the year.